SEMPER·FIDELIS

CLIFFORD HENDERSON

# *Devon* FAMILIES

Rosemary Lauder

HALSGROVE

First published in Great Britain in 2002

**British Library Cataloguing-in-Publication Data**
A CIP record for this title is available from the British Library

ISBN 1 84114 140 2

**HALSGROVE**
Halsgrove House
Lower Moor Way
Tiverton, Devon EX16 6SS
Tel: 01884 243242
Fax: 01884 243325
email sales@halsgrove.com
website www.halsgrove.com

Printed and bound in Great Britain by Bookcraft Ltd, Midsomer Norton

# Contents

| | |
|---|---:|
| *Acknowledgement* | 4 |
| *Introduction* | 5 |
| Acland of Columb John | 10 |
| Buller of Downes | 20 |
| Carew of Haccombe, Mohun Ottery, Bickleigh | 24 |
| Cave of Sidbury | 31 |
| Chichester of Hall and Arlington | 35 |
| Christie of Tapeley Park | 41 |
| Clifford of Chudleigh, Barons Clifford | 46 |
| Courtenay of Powderham, Earls of Devon | 53 |
| Cruwys of Cruwys Morchard | 59 |
| Fane Trefusis, Barons (Clinton) of Bicton and Heanton Satchville | 65 |
| Fortescue of Castle Hill | 75 |
| Fulford of Great Fulford | 83 |
| Fursdon of Fursdon | 88 |
| Gilbert of Compton Castle | 93 |
| Heathcoat Amory of Tiverton | 98 |
| Kelly of Kelly | 104 |
| Lopes of Maristow, Lords Roborough | 108 |
| Northcote of Iddesleigh, Earls of Iddesleigh | 111 |
| Parker of Saltram, Earls of Morley | 115 |
| Pellew of Canonteign, Viscounts Exmouth | 120 |
| Quicke of Newton St Cyres | 125 |
| Rous of Clovelly | 131 |
| Seymour of Berry Pomeroy, Dukes of Somerset | 137 |
| Stucley of Affeton and Hartland Abbey | 142 |
| Wrey of Tawstock | 151 |
| Yarde-Buller of Churston, Barons Churston | 157 |
| *Bibliography* | 160 |

# *Acknowledgement*

Very grateful thanks go to the present-day representatives of the
families of Devon, without whose co-operation this book
would not have been possible.

# *Introduction*

D o the landed gentry matter? Do they have any relevance now that the twentieth century has passed, and a new era begun?

To many people, the remaining handful of that once mighty class are of no significance, and will quickly disappear from the scene, unnoticed and unmourned. But will they – or will that handful still be with us at the end of the next millennium, if indeed any of us are still here?

Great houses and their estates have alway interested me, not least because of their air of stability in a fast-changing world, but also because of their great beauty. In such surroundings owners are still prepared to plant trees, knowing that they will grow to maturity undisturbed. In such places, the past, the present and the future, roll into one. Life is suddenly more peaceful, and yet more purposeful. In researching this book I visited all the families about whom I have written, and with nearly all of them it is this air of permanence, of belonging, of being one with their surroundings that came across most strongly. Without doubt, the landscape of Devon would look very different today if these few families had not held on to their acres with, in some cases, an unbelievable tenacity. It is only necessary to see the fate of those estates that have been sold up to realise this; neat little housing estates, business parks, golf courses, hotels or flats in the big house, and a forlorn lodge at the end of the drive.

*An owner does not want to sell. There is in this country a great love for land. It possibly is unexplainable, but it exists, and an owner inheriting land which has been in his family for generations, regards it as part of his duty to pass it on to his successor. It is not from any wish to sell that he sells, but because of circumstances over which he has no control...*

Thus wrote the twenty-first Baron Clinton a century ago. The past century has seen a great change in land ownership, and in the size of estates. Between 1918 and 1920, six to eight million acres changed hands in England and Wales – the largest change of ownership since the Dissolution of the Monasteries and possibly since the Conquest. At the end of the nineteenth century, much of the countryside was distributed between the upper

*The Royal Visit to Ugbrooke, 1899.*

Pictured (order of names unclear in original photograph caption) are: *Viscount Valletort, Hon Sir Stafford Northcote Bt, Lady Churston, Hon Derek Keppel, Lady Audrey Buller, Sir Hugh Clifford, HRH Duke of York, Lord Clifford, Duchess of Somerset, Mrs Delacour, Maj-Gen Sir F de Winton, Miss Lister, Duke of Somerset, Lord Churston, HRH Duchess of York, Lady Clifford, Lady Northcote, Lady Katherine Coke.*

classes, with around 30 peers owning over 100,000 acres, much of it in Scotland, and only three, all dukes, actually owning over 100,000 acres of English soil. We are lucky in Devon in that we have managed to keep 25 per cent of our estates still in the same families; the national figure is only 15 per cent, whilst in some counties the changeover has been far higher, and the number of estates that have been broken up piecemeal, often causing the demolition of the house, is far higher.

Is this good luck, or good management, or a bit of both? Devon has always been remote from the centre of events and the great quarrels of the nobles and the bloody battles that finished off many of the great houses, have passed us by. The trick, as several owners said to me, was to keep your head down and do nothing to attract attention until the troubles had blown over.

Land was always the base of power. It was what monarchs gave away to their supporters and their favourites. It was what a daughter was endowed with if she was to make an advantageous marriage and some of the most interesting and complex documents to survive are those relating to marriage settlements. This held good until the beginning of the nineteenth century when industry and commerce began to increase in importance.

The end of that century saw the dramatic and disastrous farming slump that in itself brought ruin to many landowners as well as their tenants. Just as today's farmer is finding himself up against foreign competition, so too did the farmers then. Faster, more reliable transport in the form of railways and shipping meant a flood of cheap corn and meat from all over the world, and the artificially protected market created during the years of war on the Continent was at an end. It was a harsh climate, and many tenant and yeoman farmers found they just could not survive. The great sell-off began. Whole estates changed hands, often at ridiculous prices, and the quiet flow of the upper classes to the colonies – always an option for a younger son – increased so that almost all of our great families have branches in Canada, South America, Australia, New Zealand and Africa. Not a few have been recalled to take up their position as head of a family they had all but forgotten.

*Sam Carew, killed in action in the First World War.*

For a class that had never thought twice about carrying out what it saw as its public duties, the onslaught of savage taxation and crippling death duties imposed upon it, seemed like an ungrateful body blow. In every war this country has ever embarked upon, the sons of the great houses have cheerfully ridden forth, from the earliest days of the Crusades when they raised and equipped their own troops from amongst their serfs and peasants, down to the Boer War when they were called upon by General Buller to help him defeat the Boers because the regular army was not so good at fighting on horseback over the South African countryside. But the tenant farmer and his landlord were – and they volunteered in their thousands, won the war for Great Britain, and those that survived came quietly home and resumed their peaceful rural lives. Up until quite recent times, it was not unusual for a landowner to raise a troop of militia, or riflemen, often equipping them out of their own pocket. But the First World War was nothing short of a holocaust for the landed gentry. The huge families of Victorian times had dwindled, and by this time there often was only one son to send. Most were slaughtered alongside many of the boys they had grown up with on their estates, as every church and war memorial so poignantly records. To many a sorrowing father, there seemed little point in carrying on. To be hit below the belt by swingeing taxation was just too much.

'Alas, how curious it is that these works of art only begin to obtain a wide appreciation when they are on the verge of being destroyed,' wrote Osbert Sitwell in 1935. The Second World War really was the final straw for many. Requisition of their homes usually meant that they were returned in a dilapidated condition, and there was neither the money nor the materials, nor even the manpower to repair them, and certainly no staff to run them.

Those that did survive both World Wars, and the agricultural depression in between, were the determined ones. That generation had never known the life of luxury, or numerous servants indoors and out and the endless round of parties, that their grandparents had enjoyed. The uphill struggle was to them the norm. They were the survivors and gradually the tide held and then turned. More leisure meant that more people got out and about, and found out what the world of the great estate was all about. 'Heritage' became a buzz word, and lo and behold, having done nothing but take away, the government very cautiously began to give a little back. Grants for new roofs, preservation, tourist facilities and suchlike, admittedly hideously hedged around with rules and regulations, but help nevertheless. Many of our country houses are open to the public as part of a Heritage scheme whereby in return for a grant, or a management scheme, or taxation relief, an owner is required to open a minimum number of days per year. Most of them say they enjoy sharing their home and history – after all, most of their visitors are genuinely interested.

The ending of the right for hereditary peers to sit in the House of Lords is a great tragedy, keenly felt by many of Devon's aristocracy. Here was an unrivalled body of men who between them had a vast fund of knowledge and experience of all countryside matters, and who were prepared to give of their time freely to debate and advise, taking always a long- term and disinterested view, making the best policies for the country as a whole. Many took their duties very seriously and sat regularly; all swept away on a tide of jealousy, leaving behind a dangerous vacuum.

And yet, everything goes full circle, and one of the strengths of the English aristocracy, unlike its counterparts on the Continent, is that it is not exclusive. Creating peerages is nothing new, and all sorts and conditions of men have been elevated, if only to the minor rank of baronet, which seems to have gone out of fashion. And what is the first thing a newly ennobled businessman or politician does? He rushes out and buys himself a country estate and learns to shoot. And if he is prepared to take his part in running local affairs, and take his turn in the often dull duties expected of a landowner, then he is quickly accepted and absorbed. It would seem that despite a century of Socialism, elevation to the peerage, a title, and an estate, is still considered to be an achievement worth striving for.

It could be said that the great estates are anachronistic, time warps that need dragging into the twenty-first century. But contrast our beautiful Devon countryside with the prairie lands of East Anglia, or the desecration of the Home Counties, and we have one good reason for preserving the country estates, and for being grateful to those who have clung to them. Those little copses and shelter belts, the pattern of hedges criss-crossing the hillside, are all allowed to remain mainly because they provide cover for game birds, but also quite simply because they have always been there. Feudal villages are largely a thing of the past, but communities that once centred around the squire still seem to hold together best, even if the figurehead has gone. Where he remains, and where the estate is still a major employer, then something of the old air of patronage survives.

Landowning by now is big business, and the son and heir is quite likely to have gone away to college to learn how to run the estate, whereas once he would have learnt from his father's 'man of business'. Now he is his own 'man of business' and quite often holds another job as well to keep the family finances afloat. But survive they have, leaner and tougher, but very much still here. There is great tenacity in the breed, as well as, it seems, great love of their own acres for some of them to have kept going against all odds, and it is with thankfulness that most acknowledge life seems, if not easier, then a little more certain. They are no longer numerous enough nor wealthy enough to be seen either as a threat or as a source of easy taxation. Their one prayer is to be allowed to get on with what they know best, looking after the countryside for the future, in the way that their forefathers have done for generations past.

# ACLAND *of Columb John*

## *Inebranlable* – Unshakeable

Considered by many to be the oldest landed family in Devon, the first reference to the Aclands comes in 1155 when they were in possession of a small estate in North Devon, once the property of Acca. Professor Hoskins, in his book *Devon*, considers that they may well have been of Flemish origin and crossed the Channel with William the Conqueror, who rewarded them with land in return for their support. And they have been in Devon ever since, accumulating lands that have passed down the continuous male line, although once or twice the thread has come dangerously close to snapping.

The Aclands have had a remarkable history, and they are fortunate in that the late Anne Acland, wife of Sir Richard, devoted her retirement to researching and writing down their story. However, it should be noted that her version differs from that recorded in *Burke's Peerage* in several instances, and perhaps most confusingly, she numbers the baronets from the first creation of 1647, whilst *Burke's* starts in 1677 when the title was reaffirmed; thus she refers to her husband as Sir Richard, the fifteenth baronet, but in *Burke's* he is the eleventh holder of the title. This account follows Anne Acland's version.

During their long tenure, the Aclands have produced an amazing variety; two of the most illustrious, both called Sir Thomas, were among the most colourful of hunting squires ever to cross the Devon or Somerset scene, giants of men who represented old England at its bucolic best. The next two generations produced thinking men, philanthropists keenly interested in improving the lot of the poor, who saw education as the best means of achieving this. Nearly all of them served in Parliament, initially because it was their duty and expected of them, latterly because they saw it as a way forward. As was to be expected, the old squires were true blue, but again, later Aclands veered away, first to Liberalism, and then to Socialism. They have ended up very much as they began, living a quiet life with a few acres in a (relatively) modest house.

*Sir John Acland, d.1554.*
Courtesy Acland family

The Aclands lived for several generations the life of quiet country squires in their manor house at Landkey, Acland Barton, which was rebuilt in the fifteenth century, frequently calling their sons either Baldwin or John. Hugh Acland, in 1585, married Margaret, the daughter of Thomas Monk of nearby Potheridge (ancestor of General Monk) and remained at Acland Barton. His Uncle John had moved south and bought the estate of Columb John in the Exe Valley. John became prominent in local government, a JP, and Sheriff in 1608, and twice sat in Parliament. He was wealthy enough to be one of those 'rewarded' with a knighthood by James I on his accession to the English throne, and was renowned for his charitable gifts which included the poor of 27 parishes and Exeter College, Oxford, where he instituted two scholarships for poor students – the first of several Aclands to be actively involved in education. He died childless in 1620 and is commemorated by a handsome marble monument in Broadclyst church, which he commissioned himself.

Hugh's son, Sir Arthur, had died in 1610 before his father, so Hugh's grandson, John, inherited both estates and decided to move to Columb John. The manor of Killerton was purchased for John's widowed mother, who remarried Sir Francis Vincent and whose daughter, Elizabeth, John later married; thus his father-in-law was also his stepfather. By the time the Civil War broke out, John and Elizabeth had ten small children, but this did not prevent them garrisoning the house for the king, or John from riding up to North Devon with 500 soldiers. During his victorious campaign at Exeter, Charles I conferred a baronetcy on John, but this was a short-lived victory. Columb John was taken as their headquarters by Fairfax and Cromwell, who quite won the heart of Lady Acland with his civilised behaviour. But the final victory of the Parliamentarians meant that fines were levied on all those who had supported the Royalist cause, and Columb John was assessed at £1727, the fourth-largest in the county.

Sir John died in 1647. Not for the last time, tragedy struck the family. The eldest son, Francis, the second baronet, died two years later unmarried and it was his young brother, John, aged thirteen, who succeeded as third baronet. Less than ten years later in 1655 an epidemic carried off no fewer than five members of the family, including young Sir John, his infant son, Sir Arthur, the fourth baronet, and two other brothers of John and Francis. It was through the line of Hugh, the youngest son of the first baronet, who became the fifth baronet, that the Acland line survived. It was only eight years since his father had died so it was as well that there were no death duties in those days. Sir Hugh was only eighteen when he inherited, and he lived to be seventy-six. During his long tenure, the family fortunes stabilised and the Aclands once again rose in prominence. Hugh married a wealthy Yorkshire girl who provided him with four sons to replenish the Acland stock. After a brief spell in Parliament, Hugh settled at Killerton, which he enlarged and turned into the principal family home. His son, John, married an Acland from Barnstaple, and it was their son Hugh, who inherited from his grandfather in 1713.

Hugh the Sixth (as the family refer to their ancestors) chose as his wife a lady whose lands were to have a profound effect on the Acland fortunes. Cecily Wroth was the daughter of Sir Thomas Wroth of Petherton Park in

*Elizabeth Dyke Acland.*

Courtesy Acland family

*Sir Thomas Dyke Acland, 7th Bt,
1723–1785.*

Courtesy Acland family

Somerset and she brought with her 2300 acres near Bridgwater, plus £12,000. But Hugh died when his son Thomas was only five. His mother, Hugh's widow, married Thomas Troyte the family chaplain and had two more sons, and all the children were brought up together at Killerton. Thomas, however, moved to Petherton when he came of age, and in due course made another advantageous marriage, to Elizabeth Dyke of Tetton, who brought the Holnicote, Pixton and Tetton estates into the family. Their children assumed the name of Dyke Acland.

The seventh baronet's well-connected wife died in 1753 shortly after the birth of her second son, leaving him a widower aged twenty-nine. Hunting had become something of an obsession with him around this time so he threw himself into the life of a country squire, hunting over his huge estates on Exmoor, and spending the entire hunting season at either Pixton or Holnicote. In 1770 his eldest son, John, married Lady Harriet Fox-Strangways, daughter of the Earl of Ilchester, and Sir Thomas settled Pixton, Petherton and Tetton on the couple, keeping Holnicote for himself. Around this time, land at Bude, Trerice and Gunnislake was added to the Acland lands, inherited from an ancestor who had married into the Arundell family. In later life, having given up his position as MFH after nearly thirty years, Sir Thomas turned his attention to Killerton. All around him his neighbours were remodelling their houses, so that Killerton seemed old-fashioned and neglected. Unusually, he began with the park, and called in Veitch, the up-and-coming Exeter nurseryman, whom Sir Thomas had first come across in London. No less a personage than James Wyatt was commissioned to design a new house, but his grand Palladian scheme, probably on a new site on top of the hill, never got any further than the drawing board, and the Killerton we know today was built on the foundations of the old original house. There was some talk of this being a temporary house until the new mansion could be built, but Sir Thomas suffered a double blow when in 1778 his eldest son died aged thirty-four leaving a son only a few months old. The following year, his beloved Holnicote was destroyed by fire, taking its contents with it, including all his hunting and racing trophies, the family silver and his collection of stags' heads, all of which Sir Thomas bitterly mourned. The Gold Cup, won in 1774 by his horse Grecian at the Haldon races, was saved, but little else. There was no more talk of grand new houses at Killerton.

Sir Thomas died in 1785, aged only sixty-three, leaving behind him a greatly enriched estate. The new house was in the current fashion, and around 500 acres had been enclosed to form the new parkland that so enhances Killerton.

The adventures of the remarkable Lady Harriet in the American War of Independence would make an interesting film. It all sounds so romantic. When her husband, John, went with General Burgoyne to reinforce British troops in Canada, she went with him, leaving her two young daughters with her mother. During the fighting she remained back 'at base' but at the first hint of injury or illness, she took off to nurse her husband, by sledge,

*Lady Harriet's journey down the Hudson River.*

Courtesy Acland family

by boat, by foot, until at last she was permitted to accompany him, even to the battlefront. What the commanding officer thought of this behaviour, or of the added responsibility she must have caused, is not recorded. When John Acland was taken prisoner at the Battle of Saratoga, the pregnant Harriet crossed enemy lines, waving a white flag, and travelled in an open boat, late at night in the pouring rain. The no-doubt astonished enemy commander allowed her to nurse her husband back to health over a period of nine weeks. The couple were back in England in time for the birth of their only son in 1778. However, despite her care, John died later that year, aged thirty-four. The next great tragedy was the death of her son, young John, who lived for only seven years, dying a few weeks after becoming the eighth baronet.

Harriet lived at Pixton, and when her daughter Kitty married the second Earl of Carnarvon in 1796, she took with her the Pixton and Tetton estates, and a considerable dowry, so that the Acland lands became divided and depleted. The Lady Harriet lived until 1815, and it is regretted by the family that they cannot claim descent from such a heroic lady.

The title passed to the younger son of the seventh baronet – the second Sir Thomas. He had been considered something of a profligate, getting through his inheritance of £10,000 in a remarkably short time. However, upon inheriting, he settled down and married Henrietta Hoare, of the banking family, who gave him two sons and two daughters. The second Sir Thomas, known like his father as 'Sir Thomas his Honour', was, also like his father a valiant huntsman, Master of Foxhounds, and, if anything even more enthusiastic than his father, abandoning Killerton in favour of Holnicote, now rebuilt. He managed to replace his father's collection of stags' heads, still to be seen in the stables there. But, in common with so many of the Acland heirs, he died young in 1794, only nine years after his marriage, leaving behind him a string of debts. Much of the Petherton estate had to be sold to meet them.

Yet again, a young boy inherited the estates and Thomas at the age of seven became the tenth baronet. It was assumed he would follow on from his father and grandfather, that he would become Master of Foxhounds and spend his life in the saddle, hunting by day and carousing by night, keeping open house for his hunting cronies, as had always been the case. But with young Thomas, the Acland history takes a new direction. He was of a more serious turn of mind, and of course, being so young when his father died, had not had time to become indoctrinated into that way of life. The Aclands had bred a man of learning and philanthropy, who chose a parliamentary career entering Parliament in 1812, one of the two members for Devon, as a Tory.

He married young, in 1808, to Lydia Hoare (a third cousin) and they raised a family of nine children. Both lived to a ripe old age. It was during their lifetime that Killerton was rescued from obscurity and turned into the house we see today. Veitch, for many years the agent, improved the grounds and laid out the beds around the house. A school was built for the village children, and Sir Thomas was one of the first landowners to provide a proper school to replace the old parish room system.

As a politician he gained a reputation for his strong speeches against slavery, against the conditions in the cotton mills, and against the savage game laws, all of which were taken for granted by his contemporaries. He was brought down by the Reform Bill, which he supported, when the Whig landslide in the ensuing general election toppled many an old landed Tory from his 'safe' seat. But he returned to Parliament in 1837 (aged fifty), standing for North Devon, which he continued to represent for twenty years. To his great delight, his eldest son Tom also entered Parliament at the same election, standing for West Somerset.

The Great Sir Thomas, as he became known, campaigned ceaselessly for better working conditions for the children of the poor and was horrified by their lack of education and religion. He also joined the African Civilisation Society which aimed to teach Africans how to farm, but life was not all philanthropy. With friends he formed the famous Grillons Club where on the occasion of its silver jubilee, 28 members consumed 100 bottles of wine, and Sir Thomas was 'forgiven by his fellow members for his unanswered correspondence, unreadable handwriting and impulsiveness because of his great generosity and integrity'.

*The Great Sir Thomas, 10th Bt.*
Devon & Exeter Institution

By 1851 Sir Thomas had 21 grandchildren and his children seemed set for successful lives. But as so often with the Aclands, it was not to last. Tom and his family were at Tetton when an epidemic of scarlet fever struck; one of his children died, followed by his wife Mary. To get away, Tom and his remaining five children fled to Holnicote, and for the second time in its history, the house burnt down. That same summer, Tom's brother Leopold, lost his wife to TB, so that there were two large motherless families of young children. To enable Lady Acland to care for them all, Sprydon, near Killerton, was purchased for Tom and his family. Only five years later in 1856, Lady Acland died suddenly. She and Sir Thomas had had a long and happy marriage, and he was grief stricken, visiting her grave at Columb John daily. He retired completely from public life, and as an acknowledgement of his considerable service, a statue to him was erected in Exeter. Sir Thomas spent most of his time at Killerton, with occasional visits to the house he had built for the family at Bude; he had been a keen yachtsman in his younger days. The grounds at Killerton became a great interest and it was at this time that the Veitch brothers were sending back seeds of all kinds of exotic plants from their plant-hunting expeditions, many of which flowered for the first time at Killerton, and which included the first-ever seeds of the Californian redwood trees. The Killerton Oak, as he was known, lived on, keeping a benevolent eye on his family, dying in his chair in 1871. He was eighty-eight, and 'his death left a gap in the Devon landscape as if a tree had fallen'.

*Thomas Dyke Acland, later 11th Bt.*
Courtesy Acland family

Thus Tom became Sir Thomas the Eleventh, aged sixty-two on his father's death, so that for most of his life he had been guided and overshadowed by that giant of a man, with little or no independence. His marriage to Mary Mordaunt had been frowned upon because of her family's High Church views and a legal career had been denied him because his father could not see the need for it as he would be inheriting the estates. Instead, Tom had turned his attention to education. Much of the foundation of the present education system owes itself to Thomas Acland. At that time only one child in eleven went to school and then learnt very little. The first experiment of providing a school at Killerton had proved successful, and Tom sought to spread the idea. With the help of a colleague, he drew up proposals for a nationwide scheme, on a diocesan basis, each with a training college for the teachers. Church elementary schools already existed and each parish would organise secondary schools. The bishop would head the Board of Education. By 1839, 16 diocesan boards were in existence and the first two teacher training colleges were open, at St Mark's in Chelsea and St Luke's in Exeter. The idea caught on like wildfire and Tom found himself travelling all over the country advising and encouraging. He had at last been permitted to marry Mary Mordaunt, and eventually they had a family of ten children. During Parliament, they lived in London, but during the recess they moved to Killerton, Holnicote or Bude.

Tom Acland was a man of great moral stance and courage. Association with his tenants convinced him that 'protectionism' – the Corn Laws – supported bad practice and inefficient farming methods, keeping the labourers in extreme poverty. Going against the party wishes, and those of his own supporters, Tom voted for the Repeal in 1846, and found that at the next general election he was dropped as a candidate. He threw himself into his next project, agriculture, with characteristic thoroughness. In order to ensure that he knew his subject, Tom attended a series of lectures, and then made a successful bid to prepare a report on Agriculture in the County of Somerset, which was duly published in the Royal Agricultural Society's journal for 1850. That summer, the Society brought its annual show to Exeter, bringing with it new machinery and implements which were demonstrated in the showyard at St Leonard's. This was something of an eye-opener to the backward farmers of the area, and Tom realised that such shows offered a great opportunity. He was largely instrumental in the founding of the Bath and West Society and in the setting up of its annual shows, the first being held at Taunton.

But this was the year of the tragic loss of Mary and their youngest child, and for a while Tom's life was taken up with domestic matters. He was helped by Mary Erskine, a friend of his wife, whom he married five years later and who had gradually assumed responsibility for the young children. Within five days of their marriage, Lady Acland senior died and Mary found herself looking after a distraught husband, her own family, and two other sets of motherless Acland children.

Tom became aware of gaps in the education system in that the families of the middle class were left out. Lord Fortescue had set up an agricultural school at West Buckland, but Tom was more in favour of a general education and thought that a common standard was required. Not many school-children know that it is to Tom Acland they owe the annual misery of the examination system. A local experiment was set up at Exeter, which was enthusiastically greeted by the teachers who were roped in to draw up a syllabus and prepare exam papers. On 17 June 1857, 107 candidates travelled voluntarily to Exeter to sit examinations. It was agreed that a national body was required to take the idea further but neither Church nor Government were considered suitable. The universities became the ideal choice, and so it remains.

This energetic man next turned his attention to organising his neighbours and tenants into a mobile force, in answer to the threat of a possible invasion from Napoleon III. The Devon Mounted Rifle Volunteers answered the need, and apparently they all had great fun, practising in the rifle ranges, camps in the woods and marching up and down the drive. But of course, they never saw action.

Politics had continued to be an interest, and Tom had stood unsuccessfully as a Liberal Conservative. He was once again in Parliament in 1865, and in the general election of 1868 stood as a Liberal for North Devon. Gladstone, a lifelong friend, was swept into power, and it was a disappointment to Tom that he was not offered a post. He would have seemed an obvious choice for Education, but he served on the back-benches for eighteen years.

On the death of 'old Sir Thomas' in 1871, Tom had found himself almost reluctantly the new Sir Thomas the Eleventh. He was reluctant, also, to move from Sprydon which had been home for so long, but with the death of his most dashing son Gilbert, the family moved to Killerton in 1875. Tom, at last, could put into practice some of his innovative agricultural ideas, and devoted himself to the estates. This involved a kind of 'royal progress' around the estates so that Christmas was spent at Holnicote, then Killerton until Easter with Sir Tom in London for Parliament some of the time, then the family went to London for July, Killerton again for August, then Holnicote for September and half of October, a fortnight at Bude, and back to Killerton again until Christmas when the whole cycle began again.

A programme of renovation and repairs to the estate farms and cottaages was embarked upon so that at the end of his twenty-seven-year tenure the estates were greatly improved, and free from debt. He also set up reading rooms and men's clubs and it could be said of him that he put his tenants' and workers' interests before his own. Gladstone made him a Privy Councillor in 1883, but Tom consistently refused the offer of a peerage – honours, he said, were not in his line. It was a moment of great pride for him when, in the election of 1885, two of his sons joined him in the House of Commons. 'Aclands are Trumps!' wrote Gladstone.

But as the century was drawing to a close, so, too, was the golden age of landlords, and of the Aclands. Mary died in 1892, and Sir Thomas the Eleventh, in 1898. This exceptional and admirable man was universally mourned. Shops shut in the city of Exeter, and by the time his funeral reached Columb John, it was estimated that 3000 people were crowded into the fields.

Charles, the eldest son, decided to be known as 'Sir Thomas the Twelfth', principally because there had been a Sir Thomas for one-hundred-and-fifty years. He followed his father as an excellent landlord, and at this time he was the second largest owner in Somerset with 16,000 acres, and among the top ten in Devon with 15,000 acres and 5000 in Cornwall. He waited until he was thirty-seven before marrying and his choice was Gertrude Walrond of nearby Bradfield whom he married in 1879. She was very beautiful and elegant, and together they set about refurbishing Killerton which had not been touched during his father's time. Gertie wanted everything that was fashionable and a home suitable for the large house parties that were becoming an essential part of high society. It is estimated that they spent £8000 on the house at a time when a labourer's wages were ls 8d per day.

*Sir Charles Thomas Dyke Acland, 12th Bt.*

Charles was also a barrister, a JP, and Deputy Lieutenant for both Devon and Somerset. He was a warden for the Stannaries, and his parliamentary career spanned thirteen years, during which time he was Under-Secretary to the Board of Trade and Parliamentary Church Commissioner. He was a staunch Liberal throughout his life, and continued his father's interests in the agricultural shows and in land management. In 1905, he and Gertie gave a garden party at Killerton to celebrate their silver wedding. She had greatly improved the gardens, with the rhododendron glades and the terrace in front of the house, and the sun shone on 800 guests partaking of luncheon and tea. But they had no children, and Charles knew it would be his brother Arthur's son, Francis who would eventually inherit. He made a dramatic decision.

He gave the estates to the National Trust, who wrote a letter to *The Times* on 22 February 1917, the same issue that carried news of the Raid at Ypres and listed the 1620 killed, wounded or taken prisoner there. The Trust announced that Sir C. Thomas Dyke Acland Bt had for some time been anxious to safeguard this beautiful countryside (of Exmoor) and had approached the Trust to see whether a scheme could be set up 'which would not deprive him or his successors of their enjoyment of the property'. The Trust was not to become the owner, but was to lease most of the

Exmoor estate for five-hundred years, and Sir Thomas would continue to receive the rents etc.

Charles's brother, Arthur, was of a very different mould. He had originally been destined for the Church and shocked his entire family when he announced his intention not to take Holy Orders only weeks before his ordination. Gradually he grew apart from Charles, and the patriarchal system which had so ruled his own life held no interest for him. Oxford drew him and for a time he and his wife Elsie earned a living teaching. Neither cared for pomp or extravagance and they were always poor. With his brother and father, he was an MP, and under Gladstone's administration became Minister for Education. He was a fine politician, in his element in the House, and became a great supporter of the Co-operative Movement. Only his indifferent health held him back from greater achievements.

It was whilst spending a holiday at their small cottage in North Wales, that Arthur decided to support a penniless and unknown candidate, called David Lloyd George, who was triumphantly elected for Caernarfon Boroughs. Arthur worked unceasingly both on the Welsh Board of Education as Chairman, and in the House, which exhausted him. After three years in Opposition, he decided to resign following his father's death in 1898.

There was a certain amount of resentment between the brothers, Arthur feeling that as he was, in effect, bringing up Charles's heir, some financial assistance would not come amiss. This was Francis, his eldest son, who was a welcome visitor at Killerton, but Arthur and Elsie were never comfortable there. When Charles died in 1919, Arthur became the thirteenth baronet, but remained in London. Francis, too, followed the family tradition of entering Parliament as a Liberal and became Financial Secretary to the Treasury and a Privy Councillor. But the decline of the Liberal Party meant long years on the Opposition benches, and Francis was one of the

*The late Sir Richard and Lady Acland at Sprydon.*

Courtesy Acland family

remaining Liberals in power between the Wars. Also in the family tradition, he was a keen plantsman, supporting Kingdon Ward's plant-hunting expeditions and adding to the collection of rhododendrons at Killerton. His wife, Eleanor Cropper from Kendal, was also a keen Liberal supporter and President of the Women's Liberal Federation for many years, even standing as Liberal candidate for Exeter. They had three children, Richard who succeeded as fifteenth baronet, Geoffrey who ran the family paper mill near Kendal, and Cuthbert who was the National Trust's land agent in the Lake District for twenty-five years, and an acknowledged photographer.

Sir Richard succeeded his father in 1939. He had already followed him into Parliament as Liberal member for North Devon, but during the war he formed his own 'Common Wealth' party, supporting common ownership of land. The Labour landslide in 1945 left Richard without support and he joined them as member for Gravesend in 1947. Like so many of his forebears, Sir Richard Acland was a man of principle and he resigned in 1955 over the issue of H-bomb manufacture. He took up a teaching career instead, first at Wandsworth Comprehensive, but latterly at St Luke's College in Exeter, with which the Aclands had for so long been associated. He married Anne Alford, an architect who devoted most of her career to local government before specialising in designing schools and buildings for the handicapped. She later spent much time researching the history of the Acland family, producing a book *A Devon Family*. They had three sons, John born 1939 and his two brothers, both of whom live in America.

It was Sir Richard's decision in 1944 to give all the Acland lands at Killerton and Holnicote to the National Trust, retaining only Sprydon where the family still live. John inherited the title in 1990. He is now divorced from his wife Virginia and lives in Cambridge, where he studied. He has three children, and several grandchildren.

◇◇◆◇◇

# BULLER *of Downes*

## *Aquila non capit muscas* – An eagle does not catch flies

I t sometimes happens, somewhat unfairly, that a family is remembered because of one member, more illustrious than the rest. The Buller family have been landowners and lords of the manor of Crediton since the seventeenth century. Their history begins with Moses Gould, a wealthy Exeter merchant owning a considerable amount of land and property in the city. At some stage he moved away to Dunscombe, still a farm on the estate, and in 1692 built the house known as Downes on the outskirts of Crediton. His son married Elizabeth Quicke from nearby Newton St Cyres, and their daughter married James Buller in 1739. He preferred to live on another of their estates at King's Nympton, where in 1746 he built a beautiful small Palladian-style villa known as King's Nympton Park. The Buller family originated near Looe in Cornwall, and James's mother was the daughter of Bishop Trelawny, one of the seven bishops imprisoned in the Tower of London by James II, and immortalised in the Cornish song 'And shall Trelawny die?' He survived to flourish under the Protestant William and Mary.

*James Buller (1740–72)*

Henry Parker Esq

Successive members of the family served as Members of Parliament, including James Buller (1740–72) who married Husey Gould (confusingly from a Dorset family), maintaining the status of country squires in the original house built by Moses Gould. He had chosen his site well, and although the house has been much altered, its main windows still look down the valley to the River Creedy. In the 1790s the red-brick facade was faced with Beer stone and the pediment and Buller coat of arms added, at a cost of £227 10s. The main alterations occurred when James Wentworth Buller inherited in 1827, aged twenty- nine. He was an active and prominent member of the family, and was to sit as Member of Parliament for Exeter from 1830–35, and for North Devon 1857–65. He was a Doctor of Civil Law, a Colonel of the local militia and Deputy Lieutenant, and he wanted his home to reflect his rising position. It was a time when most landowners were 'improving' their homes and James Buller employed Decimus Burton to draw up plans to bring Downes up to date. However, with the end of the Napoleonic Wars in 1815, finances were somewhat straitened with the loss of lucrative army contracts, and what was eventually built was much more modest in scale. However, as his family was steadily increasing to a total of l2 children, more space was needed, and

*Husey Gould, m.1768 James Buller.*

Henry Parker Esq

two large service and bedroom blocks were added to the rear, later demolished as surplus to requirements. Internal alterations were also carried out, principally relocating the entrance hall. The next Buller, James Howard (1835–74), gave Downes a high, heavy Victorian overcoat with tall chimneys, altered roofline, a part-Gothic extension, plate glass windows and a facing, to the rear, of shiny white bricks, removed at a later date.

The interior of Downes has some very fine features, and for the first time there are plans to open to the public. The southern front contains the old entrance hall, a pleasant panelled room with a magnificent staircase hall off it, with decorative plasterwork, a rare survival of the work of the Abbott family, with garlands of fruits and flowers suspended by means of copper wiring. Adjoining is the 'panelled room' with an early carved overmantel dated 1604 and possibly removed from Dunscombe Farm. An entire room is given over to a museum displaying many objects belonging to the Buller family and in particular commemorating Sir Redvers Buller, of whom there are many portraits and artefacts throughout the house.

Redvers, born at Downes on 7 December 1839, was the second of three sons born to James Wentworth Buller, and had a typical upbringing, going away to school at the age of eight, with holidays spent at home learning estate skills from the gamekeeper, farmers and the local blacksmith. It was whilst returning for the holidays from Eton when he was sixteen that he suffered the traumatic shock of his mother's death. She had come to meet him at Exeter Station where she developed a haemorrhage to the lung. For three days she lay on an improvised bed in the waiting room, too ill to be moved, and young Redvers never left her side. From Eton he was gazetted into the 2nd Battalion of the 60th Rifles in 1858 and rose steadily, seeing service in India and China, where he saw his first action. It was recorded of him that he was a strong character, fond of a dispute and laying down the law, nicknamed Judge Buller – an ancestor had been a judge, fond of quoting, 'the greater the truth, the greater the libel.' He quarrelled constantly with his commanding officer in China, but was popular with his men who were devoted to him, and it was this ability to endear himself that stayed with

*General Sir Redvers Buller.*

him throughout his career. His was the last regiment to leave Peking and was cut off by ice. The company was forced to overwinter there, losing 101 officers and men before it was possible to set sail for England, and then the ship was nearly lost in a hurricane. Several happy years followed in Canada before being posted to Ashanti under the command of Sir Garnet Wolsey who said of him:

*Endowed with a mind fruitful in expedients, he inspired general confidence and thoroughly deserved it. Had a thunderbolt burst at his feet, he would merely have pushed away the earth without any break in the sentence he happened to be uttering.*

Buller became head of the Intelligence department and was frequently mentioned in despatches. However, it is for his African campaigns that he is chiefly remembered and which gained for him his reputation and fame. In 1878 he took up command of the Frontier Light Horse. Again and again despatches show him leading his men, inspiring them with his own cool actions, and again and again, ignoring all danger, returning to recover wounded men. It was for one such action that he was awarded the Victoria Cross in 1879. On his return he was summoned to Windsor Castle and made an Aide-de-Camp to Queen Victoria. The second Zulu War saw him returning to Africa as Deputy Adjutant General in 1881. That year he married Lady Audrey, widow of Hon. Greville Howard, and was almost immediately sent to Egypt where although too late to rescue General Gordon at Khartoum, he did manage to bring the survivors and the rescue force, over 10,000 men, safely back to base at Korti.

The story of his wartime expeditions and exploits read like a *Boys' Own* hero; ripping yarns of daring missions and near disasters, victory snatched from defeat, death defied on several occasions, and through it all, the calm, unruffled heroic figure of Buller, his leadership unquestioned, his authority complete. He was made a Lieutenant-General in 1891, and reorganised the supply and transport depots at home which he saw as vital to any army presence abroad. In 1899 he was appointed Commander-in-Chief for the ensuing war with South Africa and he left London amidst scenes of enthusiasm and optimism, which apparently he did not share. Although it is the relief of Ladysmith that is written in the annals of British military history as one of the great feats of all time, Buller considered his primary aim was to save the two colonies of Natal and Cape. His success was undoubted and he managed to surprise the Boers, who thought themselves unassailable – except by Buller. He was given a stirring farewell from all the troops left behind and was generally considered the saviour of the Transvaal, and that his attention to morale and to such basics as canteens and hospitals played no small part in this success.

A hero's welcome awaited him on his return to Southampton, where he was given the freedom of the city and showered with honours and congratulatory addresses; in the museum room are several books full of signatures, one with 20,000 names, and an amazing collection of souvenir mugs, trays, tea caddies and the like, all commemorating the local hero. Fame, however, is a tricky thing and before long the nation's gratitude was forgotten and he found himself suspended on half-pay from his command at Aldershot, pending an inquiry into an unprepared speech he had made in an unguarded moment. Sir Redvers retired to Downes where he was greeted enthusiastically, and an equestrian statue of him was erected, a rare honour during a man's lifetime. The family have photographs of it arriving at Exeter Station, carefully secured onto a wagon, and it was placed on its plinth on St David's Hill amidst great ceremony. There it still stands, sometimes with an additional traffic cone atop his plumed helmet, sometimes without. A change of government in 1906 saw him treated with the respect he deserved, although he had had to face a Royal Commission. He spent the last years of his life happily entering into the life of a country squire, and in 1908, knowing his end was near, remarked, 'I am dying, well I think it is time to go to bed now.' Thus died a remarkable man, and among the many tributes paid to him was one from his old enemies, the Boers. General Buller's decorations included the VC, GCMG, KCB, KCMG, GCB, CB and PC.

His funeral was remarkable. The two miles of road from his home to Crediton church were lined with mourners, thousands crowded into the church and churchyard, and it was described as very solemn, very splendid, and very stately. Sir Redvers had inherited Downes on the death of his brother, James Howard, in 1874. He had one daughter, Georgiana, who never married but is recorded as 'devoting her life to the disabled' for which she was awarded the DBE.

As there was a male entail, the youngest brother Tremayne, succeeded, dying in 1917. He had three sons and three daughters, the eldest of whom was Mowbray. On Mowbray's death in 1948, Downes passed to the youngest brother Michael, as Eric, the middle brother had inherited Hunstrete in Somerset and given up his right to Downes. On his death in 1975, the estate reverted to Rosemary, the daughter of Mowbray and Silvia Watney, as the eldest daughter of the eldest brother. Unfortunately, the contents were not so protected, and Michael's daughter took what she wanted and auctioned the rest, so that when Rosemary, who had married Peter Parker, moved back, she inherited an empty house and the death duties. Mrs Parker's husband was a descendant of the Earls of Macclesfield, and together they surveyed the empty house, which no one had cared for properly for a long time, and which was threatened with a bypass across the front lawn. There was a very large question as to whether to sell or not, but in 1976 the family moved into the gardener's cottage and the long process of restoration began. Rosemary Parker managed to buy back some of the family portraits at the auction, deciding these were more important than the furniture. The roof was relined and releaded, and the ugly servant's wing knocked down.

Downes now seems set to enter a new and prosperous phase of its long existence. In 1991 Henry Parker married Susan Alvin, and his mother Rosemary lived long enough to see the birth of her two grandchildren, Redvers, and Stroma.

# CAREW *of Haccombe, Mohuns Ottery, Bickleigh*

## *nil conscire sibi* – Conscious of no guilt

This once prolific family has featured prominently in the history of Devon, and at one time there were at least five flourishing branches. The Carews were a warrior family, with a seemingly unending supply of knights ready to go off and fight for their king. Their heyday was the Tudor and Elizabethan era, when Carews were active on land and sea, and their possessions were many, but by the end of the eighteenth century their days of glory had departed.

The Carews are descended from one Walter FitzOther, Castellan of Windsor Castle and Keeper of the Great Forest there in the time of the Conqueror. As tenant-in-chief he held lands in five counties directly from King William, and had the important charge of caring for the royal brood mares so was obviously high in the favour of the king and may well have originated in Normandy.

His youngest son, Gerald Fitzwalter married the Welsh princess, Nest, daughter of Rhys ap Tudor Mawr, Prince of South Wales and she brought the lands of Carew in Pembrokeshire as her dower. The story goes that she bore him five children but such was her great beauty that both she and the castle were captured by a Welshman, by whom she had a further two children. Her Norman lord, who had probably been away fighting, recaptured his wife and lands on his return and killed the Welshman. This may, or may not be true, but it was a descendant of this marriage, Sir Nicholas, who, in the late thirteenth century, built the Early English Carew Castle in Pembrokeshire, now a ruin, and who married Amicia Peverel, heiress to West Peverel and Mamhead. Their son, Sir John (d.1324), also married an heiress, Eleanor Mohun who brought the Mohun lands at Mohuns Ottery, Stoke Fleming, Monketon and Galmpton. But Eleanor died in 1300 leaving an only son Nicholas, who died shortly after his father in 1324. Sir John's son by his second wife, Joan Talbot, also called John, inherited and was granted by his half-brother Nicholas the right to quarter the arms of the Mohuns of Devon. By virtue of his marriage to Margaret Mohun, daughter of Lord John Mohun of Dunster in Somerset, Sir John also inherited the Devon Mohun lands of his father's first wife, Eleanor, daughter of Mohun of Dunster, who thus hoped that the Mohun lands would be kept intact for his grandchildren.

This Sir John served his king well, fighting valiantly in France where he was knighted after the Battle of Crécy. His eldest son was killed at the Siege of Calais in 1347, so it was the second son, Leonard, who succeeded in 1362. He also served in France under the Earl of Pembroke, presumably on account of the Pembroke lands held by the Carews, and it is thought that he died there in 1369, leaving an infant son of two, Thomas, to succeed him.

Baron Thomas Carew (1367–1431), was still influential in Wales and was entrusted with the protection of South Wales during Glendower's rebellion against Henry IV, and distinguished himself at the Battle of Shrewsbury in 1403, considered the most ferocious battle on English soil since the Conquest, from which Henry emerged victorious. The grateful monarch rewarded Thomas with the right 'to take game from any forests, parks, chaces and warrens of the king whenever he may pass by them, and by the supervision of the keepers, verderers, foresters or officers of the same may take two or three courses after the deer'. At a time when the game laws were rigidly enforced and the royal forests jealously protected, this must have been a singular honour for the family, though possibly some kind of payment was required by the Crown.

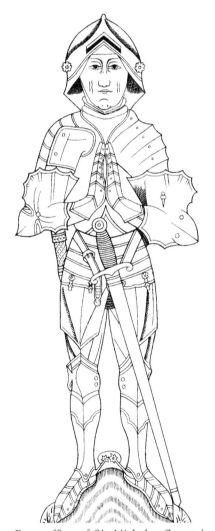

Sir Thomas continued to serve Henry V as Captain of the fort of Harfleur and defended the passage across the Seine. Later he safeguarded the passage of the Emperor Sigismund in 1416 by patrolling the seas with 300 men-at-arms.

Many of the Carews seem to have been adept at negotiating advantageous marriages, and both Sir Thomas and his son Nicholas improved the Carew fortunes considerably, he by marrying in 1380 a daughter of Sir William Bonville of Shute, and more importantly Nicholas by marrying Joan, daughter of Sir Hugh Courtenay, in 1425. This marriage was arranged by Sir Thomas who had to pay the sum of 100 marks to the Treasury (Joan was a ward of the Crown), to confirm that Joan was the co-heiress of her late mother, Philippa L'Erchdekne, but not of her father Sir Hugh Courtenay. And indeed it was from Joan's mother that the various manors and lands passed to the children of the marriage and laid the foundations of the various branches. Nicholas is described as 'of Haccombe', Sir Thomas, the eldest, 'of Mohuns Ottery', from whom descended the Totnes branch, Alexander 'of Antony', Hugh 'of Lynham' and William of 'Carew Castle' and 'Crowcombe'. Thomas died four years before his mother in 1461, leaving a seventeen-year-old son who was made a ward of the Crown. By now the family was one of the most powerful in the county, with vast possessions in both Devon and Cornwall and to safeguard this, Joan, a far-sighted and capable woman, divided her lands between her surviving sons. She herself had remarried in 1450 to Sir Robert Vere, who was slain fighting for the Lancastrian cause in 1461, and Joan was careful to leave nothing to chance as far as the L'Erchdekne manors were concerned.

*Brass effigy of Sir Nicholas Carew in Haccombe Church.*

*Sir Nicholas Carew of Haccombe,
d.1469.*

Devon & Exeter Institution

*Sir Thomas Carew, d.1586 of gaol
fever. Fom a brass effigy in Haccombe
Church.*

*Thomas and Anne Carew, d.1656.
From a brass effigy.*

## THE HACCOMBE CAREWS

When Nicholas of Haccombe, Joan's eldest son, died in 1469, he left a son, John, aged only four, who had been married whilst young to his guardian's daughter, Agnes Crocker, a not uncommon event. She died without children and John remarried but died, aged thirty-four, leaving a family of small children, the youngest of which, John (b.1501), duly inherited. In the service of Henry VIII, he was sent to join the Anglo-French force marching on Rome to release Pope Clement who had been imprisoned by the Bourbons. However, he managed to bribe his way out and Carew and his men marched south to overwinter at Naples. Unfortunately for them, the plague came with the spring and wiped out most of the force, including young John Carew. He left a nine-year-old son, Thomas – who also married young the daughter of his guardian. Marriage to one's guardian's daughter seems to have been quite the norm. By the time he inherited, life was more peaceful and Thomas had a long, but eventful life. He served as High Sheriff in 1573, by which time Elizabeth was queen, but found himself in danger because of his 'corrupt religion'. A sensible man, he put in an appearance at his parish church on Maundy Thursday, and was restored to his position as Commissioner of the Peace. However, he later died of the fever contracted at the Black Assize of 1586 which he attended in that capacity. But he had managed to reach the age of sixty-seven and his son, William, was almost elderly at thirty-eight when he inherited.

William appears to have differed from his forebears; his Catholicism led to his imprisonment for a time in 1582, and in 1599 he sold his inheritance to his youngest brother John for £1500. His other two brothers both died unmarried. It was John, therefore, who held the manors of Haccombe, and Manadon on the outskirts of Plymouth. He appears to have led a peaceful life, dying in 1626, aged forty. His son was another Thomas, who married his relation Elizabeth, daughter and co-heiress of Sir Henry of Bickleigh, and from whom is descended Sir Rivers, the present baronet.

## THE MOHUNS OTTERY CAREWS

As a boy of six, Sir Edmund inherited Mohuns Ottery in 1470. During his minority, Carew Castle was mortgaged to Sir Rhys ap Thomas, and Edmund was married off to a daughter of Edward IV's attorney general. Nevertheless, when Henry Tudor landed in Wales, Edmund joined him at Bosworth and was knighted there following Henry's victory. Such was his favour with Henry VII that he granted to him for life:

*the forests and chaces of Exmore in the county of Devon, and Rache in Somerset, with all deer therein and all courts and profits of courts, and swain motes, fines, herbage, pannage and agistments at a yearly rental of £46 l3s 4d with licence to hunt the deer, stags and buck and does, with dogs, greyhounds, bows and arrows and other instruments of the chase, provided that at his death there be one-hundred deer left in the forest of Exmore and two-hundred in that of Rach.*

He was killed in 1513 when, at the age of forty-nine, he accompanied

Henry VIII's army to France and was struck by a stray cannon ball whilst conferring in his tent with other English leaders prior to what became known as the Battle of the Spurs. He was the second Carew of his generation to be killed fighting for Henry VIII. Unfortunately, Sir Edmund left behind him a large family, and all the unpaid expenses incurred by equipping himself and his retinue for the French expedition, and this meant it was not possible to redeem the mortgages on Carew Castle.

Of the next generation, Sir Peter of Mohuns Ottery, and his uncle, Sir Gawen of Wood, near Kentisbeare, were prominent members of the court. Sir Peter and Sir Gawen were sent by the king to try to pacify the rebellion known as the Prayer Book Rebellion of 1549, when trouble flared at the remote Dartmoor parish of Sampford Courtenay against the enforced introduction of the new prayer book, written for the first time in English. The rebels marched on Crediton where they were joined by a contingent from Cornwall and it was there that the Carews were sent in an unsuccessful peacemaking attempt. The rebellion was savagely quashed on the outskirts of Exeter later that year.

It was Sir Edmund's younger son, Thomas (d.1546), who married the heiress of Bickleigh Castle, a Courtenay, with whom he was supposed to have eloped. She was under the guardianship of Thomas's elder brother, Sir William, who perhaps had an eye to the heiress himself, but instead:

*…being much in her company it was not unlikely that Thomas should fall in love with the accomplished and lovely girl. Their hearts being united, they took an opportunity of forming a clandestine marriage. Taking advantage of a dark night, she fled from the house of her guardian. So enraged was William that he sent his brother to the Battle of Flodden Field, where he acquitted himself exceedingly well.*

Thomas later found himself returning aboard the *Mary Rose*. Another brother, George, became Dean of Windsor.

Of Sir William's three sons, Philip became a Knight of Malta and was slain by the Turks, who drowned him in a sack according to family tradition. His brother, Admiral George Carew attained a kind of immortality by being aboard the *Mary Rose* when she sank off Portsmouth Harbour with the loss of 700 men in July 1545. The 'Army by Sea' was under the command of Admiral John Dudley with Carew in charge of the 'Voward' flank. The *Mary Rose*, by then an ageing vessel first commissioned in 1510, was captained by Roger Grenville (father of Sir Richard) and had fired at the French from the port side. As she turned, preparatory to firing from the starboard side, she rolled over and the sea flooded in through the open gun ports. The family still mourn the loss of a golden chain given to the Admiral by Henry VIII as a mark of his office, and a considerable amount of family pewter and possibly silver plate that went to the bottom with him. When the *Mary Rose* was raised in 1982, a sliver of wood from the hull was presented to Haccombe church and was inserted into the cross in the church.

Sir Peter the youngest brother, sold Mohuns Ottery in 1563 and moved to

*George Carew, Earl of Totnes.*
Devon & Exeter Institution

*Bampfylde Moore Carew.*
Devon & Exeter Institution

*Sir Henry Carew.*

Ireland with the aim of recovering the family lands at Odrone. He died in 1575 and with him that line of the Carews came to an end. His possessions passed to a cousin, George, the son of George Carew, Dean of Windsor, Master of the Ordnance in Ireland to Elizabeth I, and later Lt-General of the Ordnance in England. As Lord President of Munster he played a prominent part in the defeat of the Spanish forces and those of the Earl of Tyrone, Governor of Jersey at the time of James I, who made him a baron. He was created Earl of Totnes by Charles I in 1625 but died without an heir.

The Carews produced one son who has attracted a great deal of notoriety over the centuries. Dubbed the 'King of the Gypsies', Bampfylde Moore Carew was born in 1690, the son of the rector of Bickleigh, and was educated at Blundell's, where he kept a pack of hounds, and where he got into so much trouble with his hunting exploits that he ran away to escape punishment. Not liking the conventional life, he embarked upon a life of vagrancy, and the tales told of his disguises and his escapades are so numerous, and so colourful it is difficult to believe them all. Could he really have disguised himself so well that he fooled his own parents when he held up their carriage to beg for money, and dined out on the story for some time after? Eventually he joined up with a band of gypsies, fell foul of the law and was transported to Maryland but somehow escaped and returned to this country, where he supported Bonny Prince Charlie in '45. Eventually he returned to Bickleigh where he died in 1758, and is buried in the churchyard without any form of headstone connecting him to his family.

Around this time the Bickleigh branch male line failed, leaving the two daughters of Sir Henry Carew, a descendant of Sir Thomas, as his heiresses. Dorothy married John Chichester of Hall in North Devon, and Elizabeth married her cousin, Sir Thomas Carew of Haccombe in 1653, thus uniting these two branches. The family took no major part in the Civil War, and at the Restoration Thomas (d.1673) was created a baronet. His only son Henry married a daughter of the first Lord Clifford but it was through his third wife, Gratiana, that the line continued, first to their son, Henry, and when he died unmarried, his younger brother Thomas, who became Sheriff of Devon in 1731. Thomas's marriage to Dorothy, daughter of Peter West of Tiverton Castle, brought that property into the family.

Sixth baronet Sir Thomas Carew had a large family of five daughters and two sons, the younger of whom, the Revd Thomas, the rector of Bickleigh, purchased Collipriest, Tiverton. The elder, Henry, married the only daughter of Walter Palk of Marley, whose family had acquired a not inconsiderable fortune made in India with the East India Company. These were the days of wealth and prosperity, when the landed gentry could afford to spend most of their time indulging in pleasurable pursuits. It was during his lifetime that Haccombe was rebuilt, not in the fashionable Palladian style as was at one time considered, but in a plain, unadorned manner, and by the time the succeeding generation had added another wing, it had around 50 bedrooms. The eighth baronet, Sir Walter, on whose horizon there were no clouds, spent his time riding to hounds, entertaining lavishly, and being very little interested in politics, either nationally or locally. It was estimated that he had an annual income of around £20,000, but he still objected vigorously to introduction of income tax at the rate of 7d in the £ in the 1840s. His reaction was to block up all the servants' windows at Haccombe to save on the window tax. He and his wife, Anne Taylor, known as 'the Lily of Devon' from nearby Ogwell House, had one son, and two daughters, Bessie, and Beatrice, known as B. When not out hunting, Sir Walter was a keen sailor and spent some of his fortune on the ocean-going yacht, the *Beatrice*. This was no ordinary toy, but a serious 100-ton vessel designed by one of the foremost designers of the day, Sir William Symonds, Surveyor to the Navy. Although this was the beginning of the age of steam, Sir Walter would have 'none of your infernal damn engines' in his yacht. She was built in Torquay, and amidst great ceremony she was launched there in 1845 by Queen Adelaide. Sir Walter duly became a member of the Royal Yacht Squadron and raced at Cowes. When in May, 1851 he heard that the 170-ton yacht *America* had arrived at Cowes and was challenging all-comers to a race around the Isle of Wight, Sir Walter immediately took off from Gravesend where the *Beatrice* was lying and sailed to Cowes. Queen Victoria had offered a cup worth £100 as a prize and there was great enthusiasm. On 15 May what proved to be the forerunner of the first America's Cup challenge, held in August at the regatta, took place. Because of the weather the original course had to be abandoned and the race was around the Warner lightship, twice round the NW Black Buoy and finishing line off Ryde Pier. Six yachts entered, the starting gun was fired at 10.30am and they were off, the *Beatrice* immediately taking the lead. But the *America* passed her to windward before reaching the Warner lightship, and kept the lead to the finish, with *Beatrice* coming second. What a pity! The race was followed by a dinner aboard the *America*; the next day Sir Walter was laid low with a violent attack of gout.

*Sir Walter Carew, 8th Bt.*

In later years he took his family and friends on several voyages, including one to Russia. The original *Beatrice* was replaced by *Beatrice II* and later with a still larger yacht, the *Evadne* which was sold after Sir Walter's death. But the era was ending, and in 1861 Lady Carew died, and twelve years later the only son, Walter, suffered serious injuries whilst hunting. He recovered sufficiently to continue with his marriage as planned, but only a year later, committed suicide, aged thirty-two. His two sisters never married but continued at Haccombe, Beatrice dying in 1919, and Bessie in 1921.

The title passed to Sir Walter's nephew Henry (b.1870), but he did not inherit the estates until the death of Bessie, by which time they were heavily encumbered, and Sir Henry also had also to find substantial death duties. Again the only way out was to sell so the properties at Marley, Tiverton and Bickleigh, in fact everything except Haccombe, went on the market.

*Sir Henry Carew, 9th Bt.*

After the death of Sir Henry, Peter Fitzwilliam Carew, grandson of Sir Walter's third brother Thomas, and his wife Joyce Fortescue, moved into Haccombe as Sir Thomas had sold his life interest to the 'old ladies' as

*Collipriest, Tiverton, 1830.*

Bessie and B were known. Peter and Joyce later agreed to sell this back to Sir Thomas and his wife, who then moved to Haccombe just as war was breaking out, not into the mansion house which was already occupied by a girls' school, but into what were originally two gardeners' cottages on the estate, where Peter's son, Rivers, came as a small boy of four, leaving when he was ten at the end of the war. Sir Rivers, who inherited in 1976 remembers the struggle his father had:

> *The estate was run down, and wartime Agricultural Committees were soon breathing hotly down landowners' necks. My father became worn out with all the problems, and in 1942 put the Haccombe estate on the market, the bulk of which was bought by a London businessman.*

The Carews finally left in 1945.

**THE STOODLEIGH CAREWS**

This minor branch of the family descended from Joan Courtenay's fifth son, William who was knighted by Henry VII. His son married the heiress of Stoodleigh and his son married the heiress of Crowcombe in Somerset, where he preferred to live. Their son, John, was knighted in 1603 and was prosperous enough to make an attempt to regain the Pembroke estates, in which he appears to have succeeded as he is recorded as living at Carew Castle and died there in 1637. He is buried in the church at Carew Cheriton nearby. His son Thomas supported the Royalist cause, and was fined the large sum of £1085 'for his delinquincy', and his brother George garrisoned Carew Castle for the king. It fell to the Parliamentarians in 1645, and subsequently became a ruin. This branch remained at Stoodleigh until the end of the eighteenth century, when together with Crowcombe and Carew Castle, it was sold.

*Muriel, wife of Charles Robert Carew, as a child with her mother Mary Heathcoat Amory.*

Near Tiverton stands Collipriest, a lovely eighteenth-century house overlooking the River Exe. This was acquired by Thomas, the rector of Bickleigh and brother of the seventh baronet. It passed to his nephew, Charles Robert Sydenham Carew (b.1853), who married Muriel Heathcoat Amory. Their granddaughter, Nichola Carew (b.1930), married Charles Breitmayer whom she divorced in 1968, later marrying Sir George Kennard, and three of her sons have assumed the name of Carew.

Lady Kennard remembers the struggle her grandfather and father had to pay death duties, and they both 'sold, sold, sold'. The Carew lands once stretched from Bickleigh almost to Newton Abbott, but all this went, the farms sold to the sitting tenants for a pittance. Her father sold Collipriest, preferring to live at Warnicombe, which was an Amory house and came to the family with Muriel Heathcoat Amory, thus it was left to her granddaughter, Nichola Kennard. So by 1942 when Haccombe was sold off, not one of the original Carew strongholds remained in the family.

# CAVE *of Sidbury*

## *'Cave'* – Beware

T he Caves first came to Devon in the middle of the nineteenth century as holidaymakers enjoying the sea at Sidmouth. The English seaside had become fashionable with the gentry, the Napoleonic Wars having closed the Continent to them for several decades. As a result, all kinds of unlikely fishing villages suddenly found themselves becoming fashionable resorts whither the upper classes flocked in the summer months. Sidmouth was one.

Mr Daniel Cave, a banker and buinessman from Bristol with a home on the outskirts of the city, brought his family to the seaside, and a few years later purchased a house in Sidmouth called 'Witheby' (now demolished). His next step was unusual, and Daniel Cave must have had thoughts of long-term occupation, for in 1853 he bought the lordship of the manor of Sidbury, together with 700 acres. The Caves have been there ever since.

The family originated in Yorkshire, from the villages of North and South Cave in the countryside beyond Hull. Not much is known of them until the fifteenth century, when one Thomas Cave was living at Leigh Sinton in Worcestershire. His descendant, Sir Richard, supported the Royalist cause and was Governor of Hereford Castle. He was killed at Naseby in 1645. His elder brother William had been fined for 'declining' the offer of a knighthood at the coronation of Charles I; perhaps he considered it would be less expensive in the long run not to be ennobled.

By the next century John Cave, the younger son of a younger son, had moved further south to Bristol, the merchant capital of the West Country. He had a house in Arno's Grove in the Bedminster area of the city and it was here that his son Stephen was born in 1763.

Stephen married Anne Daniel, whose father had property in Barbados and such was the prosperity of the family that in 1786 they opened a bank at 32 Cornhill Street. The bank prospered and formed the basis of the family wealth for many generations, and via many mergers eventually became part of the National Provincial Bank.

Stephen and Anne moved away from Bedminster and bought a property called Cleve Hill at Down End, then in Gloucestershire, and from here Stephen, and later his son Daniel, rode daily down into the city to the family bank. He was of sufficient standing to be appointed DL (an honour recently awarded to his descendant), JP and Quartermaster of the Bristol Volunteers.

It was Daniel who began the long association with Sidbury. The lordship of the manor was part of the lands granted to the Dean and Chapter of Exeter Cathedral, and in 1801 they sold this, though not the Advowson, to the Guppy family; in quick succession it passed through two other changes of ownership before settling down with the Caves. With the manor came the ancient ceremony of the Court Leet, which the Cave family have maintained ever since when, in November, the court appoints a public crier, beadle, two constables, and the pig and duck driver. The meeting is a form of village forum, and concludes with a suitable celebration.

To Daniel Cave, Sidbury was never more than a holiday base. Bristol and the banking business were his main interests, and it would appear he never even contemplated building himself a house on his newly acquired land. Like his father, he was a JP and in 1836 was appointed High Sheriff of Bristol. His wife came from Northampton, and they had a family of two sons and three daughters.

Nevertheless, possibly with an eye to the future, Daniel Cave set about adding to his core of 700 acres. He adopted a policy of buying anything that came up for sale around Sidbury, and further than that, he offered to buy the freehold of the many smallholdings that existed. For some he had to wait until the owner died or moved, but in many cases, he bought and then leased back to the original owner, who thus became Daniel Cave's tenant, farming his own land but relieved of the responsibility of maintenance. This patient policy eventually resulted in an estate of around 3000 acres, but it took fifty years to achieve, and by this time Daniel Cave had been long dead.

Stephen, the elder son, followed a political career, having first qualified as a barrister. He entered Parliament in 1859 as Conservative member for Shoreham, in Sussex, and worked his way up via Paymaster General and Vice President of the Board of Trade to become special envoy to Egypt in

*Sidbury Manor, c.1900.*

1876 when the problems of the Suez Canal required delicate diplomacy. Later he went to Paris to negotiate the fishing convention.

The policy of buying adjoining acres had continued, but it was not until 1875 that Stephen thought about building a house. Perhaps he was looking forward to retirement as a member of the landed gentry, and a manor house was required to put the finishing touch to the Caves's estate. The architect chosen was David Brandon, who was well known for his public and ecclesiastical buildings particularly in London; country houses were a new departure for him. The site chosen was secluded from the village and from the roads along the valley, but faced towards the sea and was occupied by an old-fashioned Georgian residence called 'Woodhouse', which was demolished. The building of the great Victorian house must have been the talk of the region and it was certainly a major source of employment. A workforce of some 30–50 men would walk from Sidmouth and Ottery each day, making their own bricks in a specially constructed kiln, excavating rough stone from the fields, and watching the house rise higher day by day. From the exterior, Sidbury Manor is a typical Victorian country house, irregular, high, with varying styles and shapes, and a lot of it. Internally, it is dramatic, well constructed and with everything of the best quality. The staircase hall is particularly impressive, with stone columns supporting a gallery landing to which an imposing staircase ascends, the whole with somewhat ecclesiastical overtones. Most of the principal rooms were decorated with William Morris papers and curtains, some of which survive. There was also a service wing, which was demolished in the 1960s, and a grand stable block, and to the rear, a fine series of gardens terraced into the hillside.

*Sir Stephen Cave, d.1880.*
Courtesy Sir John Cave

But Sir Stephen, as he became in 1880, never lived to do more than begin to furnish his grand new home. He fell victim to acute appendicitis and died later the same year, aged sixty. He had no children so the estate passed to his brother, Charles, who had continued in the family banking business. He and his wife were very much part of the Bristol scene; she was the daughter of Dr Addington-Symonds of Clifton, and he was a JP and DL for Gloucestershire, and served as High Sheriff of Bristol in 1863 and of Devon in 1898. He was created a baronet in 1896, in recognition of his brother's parliamentary career. By now the family bank had become part of the Union of London and Smith's Bank, of which Charles was a director, and it was not until he retired just before the First World War that he came to live at Sidbury. At that time the estate was at its peak, covering the whole valley down to the edge of Sidmouth and from Ottery East Hill to Salcombe Regis, and was around 6500 acres of fertile, well-managed farmland.

When Sir Charles and Lady Cave did eventually take up residence in their large and impressive country house, they had just a short time to enjoy the last days of the Edwardian era for which Sidbury Manor was originally planned. The Caves owned the larger portion of the village of Sidbury with over 50 cottages, and much of the valley. They must have looked forward to settling down to the life in the established pattern of shooting parties, country house balls, social gatherings and weekends, with as many staff as they needed, life as it had been for many centuries.

*Sir Charles Daniel Cave, 1st Bt.*

The Caves had three sons. Daniel, the eldest, died unmarried in 1901. His younger brother, Charles Henry, in 1892 married Beatrice, daughter of Sir Frederick Williams of Tregullow in Cornwall. Their middle son, Walter, was killed in 1915 at Ypres, on his twentieth birthday.

In 1922 Sir Charles died, and with him the Sidbury estate, which had had so short a heyday, went into a decline that has only recently been halted. Death duties caused the first sale of some of those lands so carefully acquired. Several hundred acres on the outskirts of the estate went, along with land in Gloucestershire and the house at Cleve Hill, which had been a hospital throughout the First World War. Only ten years later, the second Sir Charles died, and was succeeded by his son, Edward Charles, who had come through the war though wounded, and had married Betty Coleridge. They were divorced in 1942 and Sidbury Manor was let on a long lease to Alexandra College from Westbury-on-Sea, Essex. Another blow was dealt to the estate when Sir Edward died, aged only fifty-three, in 1946, and more land had to go.

*Sir Charles Cave, 4th Bt.*
Courtesy Sir John Cave

The family were living at Castle Hill, and it fell to the fourth baronet, Sir Charles Cave, to pull the estate together. He did this by reviewing rents, improving cottages, selling off others and seriously studying how the estate was managed. By now the family had no connections with the banking business, and Sir Charles thought it more appropriate to take a course in estate management at the Royal Agricultural College, Cirencester, where he qualified as a Fellow of the Land Agents Society. He was also much involved in local affairs and served as a member of Devon County Council from 1955–65, was High Sheriff of the county in 1969, and like so many of his family, DL. His wife, Elizabeth Gore, proved a mainspring of strength when in 1962, they took the decision to move back to the then empty manor house with their young and growing family. It was they who dramatically reduced costs by demolishing the service wing.

Sir Charles continued the family interest in forestry, planting over 100,000 trees on the estate, and laying out the beautiful grounds that surround the house. Above all, Sidbury was once again a family home. The estate had been reduced to some 2500 acres, some of which is farmed in hand, by Sir John the fifth baronet, who inherited in 1997. He, too, studied at the RAC, Cirencester and his prime interests are farming and forestry. But moving with his own young family into the house, and the increasing workload of running the estate, has meant that a farm manager is now employed. As with so many of his generation, and his father's, he has had to learn to take over the role of agent and bailiff. Sir John takes an active part in the Devon County Show, and is currently Devon branch Chairman of the Country Land and Business Association. He is the elected council member for Devon of the Royal Agricultural Society of England, and is a governor of Bicton College of Agriculture. He is continuing the forestry policy begun by his father, and is also keenly interested in the grounds, laid out from the 1880s onwards, and now beautiful with mature trees and shrubs. The terraced walled gardens suffered the neglect of wartime and school occupation, but are gradually being reclaimed. The twenty-first century will, it is hoped, be a more settled chapter in the history of Sidbury Manor.

*Sir John Cave, 5th Bt.*

◇◇◆◇◇

# CHICHESTER
## *of Hall and Arlington*
### *Ferme en foi* – Firm in Faith

The Chichesters are one of Devon's oldest, and at one time, most pro-lific families. Robert de Cicester is recorded as being granted lands in Sussex by King John, where the family continued, serving their kings in the Holy Land, in France, where Roger de Cicester was knighted after Poitiers, and against the Welsh, until moving to Somerset and then to Barnstaple in 1384 when John Chichester married Thomasine, daughter and heiress of Sir John de Ralegh. Their son, John, fought at Agincourt, and his son, Richard, was sufficiently well established to serve as Sheriff. By this time the Chichesters were a prominent family, and in 1461 another Richard married another heiress, also called Thomasine, daughter of Simon de Halle.

*Hall.*

Unlike other branches of the family, most of those who inherited the Hall estate were content to lead the life of country squires, looking after their land, hunting, shooting and playing their part in local affairs. At its height the estate ran from the east bank of the Taw towards Swimbridge, but in 1925, on the death of Charles Hamlyn Chichester, part was sold to meet death duties. Today it is about 2500 acres of rolling North Devon country-side, which has been in the family for over five-hundred years. The farms are let to tenants, some of whom have worked the same land for genera-tions. No doubt the original de Halle house underwent many changes over

*Charles Chichester, High Sheriff of Devon in 1950.*

Courtesy Mrs Maxse

the centuries and there is a picture of a delightful Queen Anne house. But in 1827 Robert and Clarentia Chichester, while on their honeymoon in North Wales, were influenced by the grand houses they saw. After he inherited in 1835, Robert succumbed to the fashion of the time and commissioned Philip C. Hardwick (whose father is best remembered for the Euston Station entrance arch) to build the present house. Unfortunately the money ran out and the Barnstaple architect R.D. Gould was asked to complete the servants' wing in the 1850s.

Today, this is the last of the Chichester houses in North Devon. Charles Chichester, who moved there as a boy in 1911, lived there until he died. The estate passed to his eldest daughter, Penelope Maxse, who lives in a more manageable ancient farmhouse lower down the valley. As a family, the Chichesters never threw anything away. When Charles died and a sale became desirable, it took five men a week to clear the cellars of artefacts going back three-hundred years. It is possible that when Robert Chichester pulled down the Queen Anne house the contents were placed in the existing cellars, the new house built on top of them, and the family took out what they needed and left the rest. The consequent sale held over three days, was the wonder of the area. Sotheby's catalogued and sold almost the entire contents.

What survives from earlier years is the delightful range of outbuildings, including a raised granary. Hall was rebuilt at a time when servants were plentiful and cheap. During the Second World War the house was taken over by a school for handicapped children from London. When the family returned the servant's wing was not reopened and remains unchanged. It is an example of how a past generation lived. But even in pre-war days, life at Hall did not consist of a ceaseless round of entertaining. The Chichesters were country squires and informal family and shooting parties were more their style. Robert and Clarentia's son Charles was typical, deeply involved in running the estate and local affairs, he was hospitable and looked after both tenants and servants well. He claimed no servant ever left his service. Although the story that he gave an annual party to Barnstaple cabbies is probably a myth, he did distribute clay pipes at Christmas, along with presents of beef to his servants and tenants. His grandson, also named Charles, continued along the family tradition. He read agriculture at Cambridge, was High Sheriff of Devon in 1950, and served as a magistrate and district councillor for over thirty years as well as acting as trustee for the Lynton Disaster Fund. During the war while he was abroad, his wife Betty and their children moved to a cottage where she took control, while he sent letters of advice from India which generally arrived months too late.

*Charles Chichester, DL, JP, son of Robert Chichester, b.1828, m.Beatrice, daughter of Sir Arthur Chichester of Youlston.*

Today the tradition continues. The land is still farmed by tenants. The house and the great hall are still used to entertain family, friends and shooting parties, when by custom, the guns and beaters all sit together. In short, Hall is still a house at the centre of a living estate.

Hall was one of three principal estates held by the Chichesters in North

Devon until 1949 when Arlington passed to the National Trust, and 1920 when Youlston, both within 20 miles of Barnstaple was sold.

*Youlston House, Shirwell.*

The main branch of the family continued at Raleigh on the outskirts of Barnstaple until the end of the fifteenth century, when John Chichester married Margaret, daughter and co-heiress of Sir Hugh Beaumont of Youlston, which had been in her family for generations. From this couple are descended all the main branches of the family. The next century saw the family firmly established and laid the foundations for its future prosperity. Hugh, son of John and Margaret, built or rebuilt Youlston, much as it is today. Amyas, a half-brother, acquired the Arlington estate and another brother founded the Widworthy branch. But it was the family of Hugh's son, John, who really raised the family profile. His wife was a Courtenay from Powderham, and they had an enormous family. Among his sons-in-law were Fortescues, a Bassett, Prideaux, Pollard and Trevelyan. Arthur, the eldest son, distinguished himself in various campaigns and was sent to Ireland as Lord Deputy, becoming Lord Chichester of Belfast in 1625, and from whom are descended the Earls of Donegal. John himself served twice as Sheriff, and twice as MP for Barnstaple and was knighted for his services. His second son, John, inherited the family estates. Youlston became the principal residence when Raleigh was sold in the early 1700s. The baronetcy had been created in 1641, and Sir Arthur, the third baronet, instituted a grand building programme at Youlston, leaving it one of the finest houses in North Devon. The Victorians thought it plain and dull, but its classical elegance has stood the test of time, and behind the plain facades are some very fine interiors with intricately plastered ceilings,

*Admiral Sir Edward Chichester.*

a room with Chinese wallpaper and a first-class example of a seventeenth-century staircase. It is a little known-gem and one can only wish that it had been Youlston and not Arlington that passed into the hands of the National Trust.

Many of the Chichester sons have served in the Army, and not a few in the Navy, but two stand head and shoulders above the rest. Sixty years separated the hero's welcome they were both given when they returned to Plymouth, home of all naval men. The first naval hero was Sir Edward, ninth Baronet of Youlston. He had already come to the attention of his naval masters when as a captain living at Instow on the Torridge estuary, with the help of a small crew, he managed to rescue a gunboat which had been driven ashore in a gale and by boarding the vessel, steered it to safe anchorage. He soon found himself in command of a troopship and by 1898 was in command of the four men-of-war sent to Manila in support of the American navy under Admiral Dewey. The German navy decided to get involved and a naval patrol was despatched to shake off the threat; but were unwilling to take on the British, so their admiral attempted some form of negotiation with Chichester, visiting him on board his ship. The encounter ranked high in naval stories for when asked by the German admiral what were his plans for the morning, Sir Edward replied, 'That is known only to Admiral Dewey and myself', a response that for a long time was much quoted. The German departed, none the wiser but when all four British ships weighed anchor and sailed in line across his bows, he took the hint and turned for home. Sir Edward was seen to have averted a potentially disastrous situation and was considered the hero of the hour in America. Back home he was highly praised and his career continued with his appointment as Admiral Superintendent Naval Establishment, and ADC to both Queen Victoria and Edward VII. He served twice in both Egypt and South Africa, and when he died in 1906 in Gibraltar, his body was brought home to Plymouth aboard HMS *Formidable* with flags and pennants at half-mast, and a detachment of Royal Devon Yeomanry joined with the Navy to bring him home to Youlston and to Shirwell churchyard.

Sir Edward's son, Sir Edward George, the tenth baronet, also served in the Navy and saw action in the South African war, and another son was lost in the Battle of Jutland.

*Francis Chichester's original 'Gipsy Moth'.*   Courtesy Giles Chichester

*Francis Chichester (on the right) and family.*   Courtesy Giles Chichester

Francis Chichester was a grandson of the eighth baronet, whose son Charles was presented to the family living of Shirwell, where Francis was brought up. He had a lifelong love of the sea, although he never joined the Navy, preferring always the challenge and excitement of pitting his own strength against the elements. He took to the air, revelling in the freedom, and was only the second person to make a solo flight from England to Australia in 1929, and the first to make the long-distance flight in a seaplane in 1931 across the Tasman Sea.

During these prolonged absences his wife was largely left to carry on the family business of publishing maps and guides, set up by Sir Francis in 1946 and still run by his son Giles. In 1958 when he was taken ill with suspected lung-cancer, his wife refused permission for a lung removal and gradually, following a regime of healthy living and plenty of fresh air, Sir Francis recovered. As part of his convalescence he took up single-handed sailing. A notice advertising a single-handed race attracted him and he decided to have a go, got himself a new yacht – and won.

He was an aviator, a navigator and a passionate ocean-racer and in 1960 won the first solo transatlantic yacht race. Not satisfied, he decided to have another go, beating his own record in 1962. His young son Giles vividly remembers the return trip sailing with his father. Alastair Cooke, the broadcaster, recalls going to greet Chichester as *Gipsy Moth III* reached the American coast in 1962, an event which attracted very little attention over there. 'A very rum sort of hero,' Cooke wrote. 'A Popeye in the flesh with a face like an ageing lobster, an iron little man imperturbable to the point of listlessness. He was totally unselfconscious, a heroic throwback, totally absorbed in whatever problem was occurring.'

*Francis Chichester.*

Giles Chichester Esq

Francis Chichester never had a great deal of capital, and home was above the shop in London and a yacht moored on the Beaulieu river. When he decided on a new yacht to sail around the world, he persuaded the 'Dulverton' relations to sponsor him; this was *Gipsy Moth IV*. The whole world followed his progress when on 27 August 1966 he set sail in *Gipsy Moth IV* on a solo one-stop global circumnavigation during which he set several speed records. He sailed for 29,630 miles alone, one of only three small boats ever to make it round the Horn. He recalled 60–80ft waves behind him and wondered what it would be like in a 120-knot wind, and completely understood why the clipper captains told their inexperienced crews never to look behind them. After a capsizing incident, it took Chichester two weeks to get things back together again. This remarkable sailor looked at the fragments of a bottle and calculated that the yacht must have turned through 131 degrees to force the bottle to fly from its niche and that the mast was therefore at 41 degrees below the horizontal. Why did he do it? To show that at sixty-five he was still capable and to prove his good seamanship, he told people.

When on 28 May 1967 Francis Chichester returned to Plymouth he was given a tremendous welcome. HM Queen Elizabeth, using the sword of Sir Francis Drake, knighted him at Greenwich later that year, and he was showered with awards and medals and dignities. In 1972 he joined his more conventional naval uncle in Shirwell churchyard, aged only seventy. Sir Francis's son, Giles, is MEP for the county of Devon.

## ARLINGTON BRANCH

The beautiful estate that surrounds Arlington has changed little, but the house itself has been rebuilt twice, first in 1790 when Col John Francis Chichester who had inherited seven years earlier, decided on a grand new house. Apparently it was so badly built that only twenty years later, it had to be demolished, and the services of Thomas Lee were called upon to design an even grander house, which has stood the test of time rather more

*Rosalie Chichester.*
Courtesy Giles Chichester

CLARISSA
CLIFFORD'S
GREAT AUNT.

successfully. Col Francis's son, John, followed a naval career before serving as MP for Barnstaple and was created Sir John Chichester, Baronet of Arlington in 1840. He was succeeded by his son Sir Alexander Palmer Chichester, second and last baronet, who had one child, Rosalie. Her mother, also Rosalie, was widowed and remarried to her husband's relative, Sir Arthur, the eighth baronet, from Youlston. Apparently both remained in their own homes and it was something of a marriage of convenience. Young Rosalie, brought up by her mother and grandmother, apparently remained in ignorance of her ownership of Arlington until her mother's death in 1908. This remarkable woman, who lived to be eighty-four, was a keen naturalist, and accomplished artist. She travelled widely and kept copious diaries from the age of thirteen. As she grew older, she retreated more and more into her world at Arlington where wildlife was encouraged, plants allowed to proliferate at will, and the whole parkland enclosed in eight miles of iron railings 'to protect the deer' – the first ever deer sanctuary. She kept Shetland ponies and Jacobs sheep, and filled the house with collections of seashells, model ships, butterflies, snuff boxes, fans and much else, and with 3470 acres the whole lot was given to the National Trust. The parkland is maintained much as a nature reserve, roamed by descendants of the original Shetland and Jacob sheep.

The distinctive emblem of a heron holding an eel adorns all three ancestral homes, usually surmounting the gate pillars, and nearly all of the Chichesters rest peacefully in the churchyard at Shirwell.

# CHRISTIE
## *of Tapeley Park, Instow*

The Tapeley estate on the Torridge estuary in North Devon has changed very little down the long centuries. It is dotted with ancient farmsteads, still surrounded by traditional farmbuildings. There is an historic quay, a long foreshore, and an attractive house overlooking it all.

The Christies came to Tapeley by marrying the Clevland heiress; that is well known and beyond dispute. But there is romance as to how the Clevlands came to live in such a beautiful place. One version is that Captain William Clevland, a Scotsman from Lanarkshire, was shipwrecked in Bideford Bay, and saw Tapeley Park as he walked up the foreshore towards Bideford. The better version states that he was sailing 'his fine vessel up the Torridge and espied Tapeley through his telescope'. Both versions agree that he announced his intention of making Tapeley his home. That was in 1702. He achieved his ambition in 1704 and Tapeley passed from the Giffards who had owned the manor since Henry VIII's time, to the Scottish Clevlands. The manor house was relatively new, described as of cob, and it basically still survives at the heart of the present house. The Clevlands settled into their new property but little is known of their early history there. During his long naval career, Commodore Clevland had taken part in many memorable actions during the reigns of three monarchs, William, Queen Anne and George I, before retiring as the first Controller of the Storekeeper's Account in the Royal Navy. In 1702 he received the Freedom of the City of Edinburgh, and of Hamilton in Lanarkshire, the year he purchased Tapeley. The following year he married Ann Davie, from nearby Orleigh Court, an old North Devon estate.

His son, John, was MP for Saltash, and Secretary to the Admiralty from 1751 until his death in 1763, so must have divided his time between London and Tapeley. Hester, his sister, married William Saltren-Willett from Porthill, across the estuary at Bideford, and it was their grandson who later inherited the Tapeley estate.

William's grandson, also John, became a director of Greenwich Hospital, and followed a parliamentary career, representing Barnstaple for over forty years. He considerably enlarged Tapeley by building on the large dining room, ostensibly for the sole purpose of entertaining his constituents lavishly, particularly, no doubt, at election times. One of his brothers Augustus Clevland (b.1754) joined the East India Company when he was seventeen and subsequently became Governor of Bengal. But the climate, as with many of his countrymen, did not suit Augustus, who died there, aged thirty. A monument to his achievements was erected in front of his former residence:

> *To the memory of the late Augustus Clevland Esq... who without bloodshed, or the terror of authority employing only the means of conciliation, and benevolence, attempted and accomplished the entire subjugation of the lawless and savage inhabitants of the Juneterry of Rajamahall, who had long infested the neighbouring lands by their predatory invasions, inspired them with the taste for the arts of civilised life and attached them to the British Government by a conquest over their minds... The Governor General and Council of Bengal in honour of his character, and for an example to others, have ordered this monument to be erected.*

*Archibald Clevland in regimental dress.*      Courtesy Christie family

Apparently he achieved this with the aid of large quantities of good British fruitcake. Several officers had failed repeatedly in their attempts to bring the Juneterry to heel, and in desperation decided to send in 'good old Gus'. He went unarmed, and unattended by a military force, but with fruitcake which he offered to the native women, talking them round whilst their men were away. He then persuaded the tribesmen that what the British really needed was a force of rangers to patrol the hills and keep order, and could they do this for him? So effectively they were patrolling themselves, and all was peace.

On the death of John Clevland in 1817, the Tapeley estate passed to his great-nephew Augustus Saltren-Willett, who assumed the arms and surname of Clevland. He married Margaret Caroline Chichester in 1830, one of the six children of John Palmer Chichester of Arlington. Augustus joined the Enniskillen Dragoons, and served at Waterloo. He died in 1849 leaving one son and two daughters. That son was Archibald Clevland who joined the 17th Lancers when he was just seventeen and was one of only three officers to survive the Charge of the Light Brigade. In the Christie archives is a long letter home recounting that disastrous engagement:

> *Lord Raglan had been told by a man who wanted the cavalry to do something brilliant, the wrong positions of the guns. He ordered us to charge... I must tell you that the guns we charged were nine 12-pounders, so you can fancy how we were mown down...*

His silver pouch box, still preserved, saved him from one cossack's lance thrust, and the tip of the next was blunt 'Was that not a lucky escape?' he wrote. But his luck ran out just one month later when he was killed at Inkerman. His mother was distraught. Her melancholy statue down by the lake at Tapeley everlastingly mourns his loss, but the more eye-catching obelisk erected to him overlooking the estuary where all could see it, was blown to pieces by a lightning bolt in 1933. The 50ft stone column was broken into fragments, the surrounding iron railings twisted and torn, and only parts of the granite base survive.

It was Archibald's sister, Agnes, who by marrying William Langham Christie, brought the Tapeley estate into that family. The Christies are of Swiss origin, and it is recorded that Daniel Christin, as his father had wasted his property, sought his fortune by joining the East India Company. He changed his name to Christie on joining the Bombay engineers, rising to the rank of major. Chivalrously, he prevented a contingent of British soldiers from robbing the ruler's harem of their jewellery, who in gratitude, fearing a different intent on the part of the soldiers, gave the gems to Christin. He was rewarded by the Sultan with a fortune of around £20,000. How he came to meet, and woo the daughter and heiress of Sir Purbeck Langham of Glyndebourne and Saunton is not recorded, but it was their grandson, Willam Langham Christie who combined the two estates.

Tapeley Park underwent major alterations when William Christie and Agnes gave it a somewhat severe, Victorian brick facade. Gone was the pretty white house that had so attracted Commodore Clevland who would not have recognised its replacement. Their eldest son, Augustus Langham Christie, married into the highest rank of county families; his bride was Lady Rosamund, daughter of the Earl of Portsmouth from Eggesford House, and granddaughter of Earl Fortescue. She had a profound influence on Tapeley, and wrote in her journal:

*When I first saw Tapeley it was in the winter of 1881 before my marriage to Augustus Langham Christie. It was a Georgian stucco house, very plain and rather dreary in appearance, for many of the front windows had been blocked and the sunk apertures painted black with half-drawn paint blinds, cords and tassells, looked very dull. The terrace walk and garden did not exist and the drive approached between iron railings.*

Lady Rosamund was to change all that.

> *I came to live at Tapeley about four years after my marriage. The house had been restored and altered by my father-in-law. It had fallen into a bad state of repair. The stucco, save on the library side had been replaced by red brick with white brick lines and the parapet removed to give place to a sloping roof. He was most forbearing in allowing us to call in the leading Queen Anne architect of the day to restore the house. During the course of many years, the house in Mr John Belcher's hands assumed its present appearance. We were unable to do the alterations all at once as we could not have faced the expense, and at the outbreak of the Great War the library side remained in dilapidated stucco. The builder, being aware that we had the plans, approached us to undertake the work on account of unemployment in Bideford. It proved one of the best strokes of business as well as a charity, for the cost was very slightly higher than before the war, and ever since would have cost much more. He stipulated that only married men should be employed. My husband never grudged money spent on the improvements or the adornment of Tapeley and the estate that he loved so dearly.*

When Belcher died Lady Rosamund placed a plaque to his memory on the wall of the house. It was obviously a long and happy relationship between

*Lady Rosamund Christie.*
Courtesy Christie Estates

him and his employers, which resulted in the greatly improved house we see today. The garden that is now such a well-known feature had its beginnings at this time with the laying out of the terrace and the borders. Lady Rosamund liked to save a little money each year to spend on Tapeley, which paid for some of the interior work, the summer house, and the long flight of steps which was another of her many bargains, for they were made of rejected gravestones originally destined for the war cemeteries. She furnished and refurbished the house, patronising the best craftsmen of her era, particularly the William Morris workshops. It is true to say that the beautiful house and gardens that attract many visitors are entirely due to Lady Rosamund.

Her marriage, however, was far from happy. Augustus's 'eccentricities' were becoming rather more serious, and eventually she banished him to the other Christie estate at Saunton. The couple had one son, John, who won the Military Cross in the First World War. He preferred to live at Glyndebourne, the Christie estate in Sussex, which his father passed over to him. His marriage to Audrey Mildmay, the opera singer, brought about a dramatic transformation when together they embarked on turning Glyndebourne into the world-famous opera house. The first performance was given in 1934, and has continued ever since with breaks in 1948 and '49, and in 1992 and '93 when the new opera house was being built.

When Augustus died in 1930, in an act of revenge on his wife, he willed Tapeley to some distant cousin in Canada. Lady Rosamund fought the will in the law courts, eventually proving that he was of unsound mind when the will was made. She finally won shortly before her own death in 1936.

*Three generations of the Christie family on the lawn at Glyndebourne 1895. From left: John Christie, William Langham Christie and Augustus Langham Christie.*
Courtesy Sir George Christie

Photographer: Guy Gravett

For several years during the Second World War Tapeley was let out to evacuee children from Plymouth, and then as a home for the Invalid Children's Aid Association, and for a spell as an hotel, before becoming the home of John and Audrey's daughter, another Rosamund. Her brother, George Christie, took over the running of Glyndebourne and was knighted in 1984.

Rosamund lived at Tapeley from the 1970s until 1988, during which time she opened the house and garden to the public, but ran everything on a shoestring, and insisted on doing almost everything herself, from taking parties round the house, to making the scones for the teas. She is best remembered for her parrot which invariably perched on her head. It is fortunate that she inherited her grandmother's love of Tapeley, and appears to have passed this on to her nephew, Hector Christie, who is the eldest of Sir George's three sons. He describes himself as a shepherd, and for many years lived at Saunton managing the farm there, but following his marriage to Kirsty MacDonald, moved to Tapeley. They have two young children, Bessie and Archie and have spent much time restoring both house and garden. Hector at one time had plans for restoring the Clevland monument but found the cost to be prohibitive. He is a keen footballer and won a certain amount of notoriety for his firm stance during the Foot and Mouth crisis of 2001 when he resisted MAFF and barricaded his property against them, seeking to protect his pedigree herd of Aberdeen Angus cattle. During more normal times, the gardens are regularly open and Tapeley makes a lovely setting for the many weddings that take place there.

*Rosamund Christie.*

The large estates at Saunton amount to some 6000 acres, now in the ownership of various trusts and companies. Much of the village of Westleigh, which originally housed the estate workers for Tapeley, is still owned by the estates. This unusual little village, with its quaint cob and thatched cottages huddled together is built in such a manner that although only half a mile from Tapeley, it is not visible from the house. Down on the Torridge, Instow was at one time largely owned by the Clevlands and Christies, and the estate owns the entire foreshore which was purchased from the Crown. It also owns the foreshore and beach across the estuary at Saunton, and the huge acreage of sand dunes behind it, some of which is leased to the MOD; the whole area is a nature reserve, between which the interests of tourism and the local population tread a wary path. It is a traditionally-run estate with tenant farmers, let cottages and forestry.

◇◇◆◇◇

# CLIFFORD *of Chudleigh*

## *Semper paratus* – Always ready

Tom Clifford, fourteenth Lord Clifford, was a boy of nine when he first visited Ugbrooke Park. He remembers standing in the courtyard with his father, looking at a scene of utter devastation. Smashed slates from the roof, fallen plaster, broken glass underfoot, rubbish and debris were everywhere, and he wondered if it could ever be put to rights. That was in 1957. Today Ugbrooke Park is one of Devon's foremost 'stately homes' and a popular visitor attraction, thanks entirely to the efforts of Tom Clifford and his father.

Ugbrooke began life as a palace of the Bishops of Exeter in 1080 and it continued to be a possession of the cathedral until 1547, when the Duke of Somerset was granted a long lease as a reward for his success in action during the Civil War. Sir Piers Courtenay was the next owner, and through the marriage of his daughter to Anthony Clifford of Borscombe in Wiltshire, the estates were much increased and amalgamated. The Cliffords are a very old family, claiming descent from the first Duke of Normandy, with vast possessions in the Welsh marches, including the ruinous Clifford Castle where Fair Rosamund, so beloved of Henry II spent her childhood. The family were powerful barons with possessions in the north, becoming Earls of Cumberland, a title dying out in the seventeenth century, when the Clifford family in Devon became the senior branch.

*Thomas, 1st Lord Clifford.*
Courtesy Lord Clifford

The power and fame of the Cliffords reached their zenith with Thomas, first Lord Clifford, born at Ugbrooke in 1630. Like his father and grandfather, he initially pursued a legal career, but in 1660, as MP for Totnes, he was in the Parliament that voted for the return of Charles II. His rise in favour was meteoric and such was his favour at court that Charles II stood godfather to Clifford's son Charles. During his career he held various government positions, was involved in naval affairs alongside the future James II, and was general commissioner of prizes taken at sea during the Dutch Wars. Thomas saw active service in the Navy for which he was knighted; and later became a Privy Councillor and Comptroller of the king's household. He was one of the inner circle that formed the CABAL, Clifford being the 'C', and was largely instrumental in the drawing up of the Secret Treaty of Dover between King Charles and Louis XIV, which paved the way for the Anglo-French war with the Dutch and promised support if King Charles ever attempted to re-establish Catholicism in England. This Treaty, written in Clifford's own hand, formerly hidden at Ugbrooke, is now in the British Library. It was for this work that Clifford was created Baron Clifford. Charles II's shrewd sense of survival soon told him that restoring Catholicism was not possible and in fact the tide was turning when a year later, the Government brought in the Test Act which required all who held office to take Holy Communion according to the rites of the Church of England. The king put off his own conversion until his deathbed, but not so Lord Clifford who quietly entered the Church of Rome and thus could not bring himself to submit to the Test Act. So, in 1673, with great dignity and courage, he resigned, aged forty-two. So concerned was the king for his safety that he issued Clifford with an unprecedented pardon for anything he may have done prior to 30 June 1673.

*Portrait of Hugh, 3rd Lord Clifford, by Hudson.*  Courtesy Lord Clifford

Lord Clifford left London to live quietly at Ugbrooke with his family. His wife was Elizabeth Martyn, co-heiress of the neighbouring estate of Lindridge. He was already suffering from ill-health, and died only four months after his resignation – of gallstones, not by hanging himself with the curtains of his bed as is suggested in some histories.

Two of Lord Clifford's sons had predeceased him at the ages of nineteen and twenty, and it was his third son Hugh, who at the age of ten inherited, the same age as his father had been when he inherited. The first Lord Clifford had begun rebuilding Ugbrooke in keeping with his new status, but never lived to see it finished, and left £2000 in his will for this purpose, being buried in his new family vault below the new chapel. But following the family's fall from power – and it was not until the Catholic Emancipation Act of 1829 that Catholics could once again hold any position in government, Army, Navy or the Church – the second Lord Clifford found his income reduced and few ways of increasing it open to him. Far from finishing the grand new house, it seems all work ceased and Hugh lived quietly content in Devon, marrying an heiress and husbanding the family fortunes until his death in 1730, aged sixty-seven.

*Hugh, 4th Lord Clifford.*
Courtesy Lord Clifford

Unfortunately for Ugbrooke, his son died two years later, leaving the fourth Lord Clifford a minor, aged five, with a devoted but spendthrift and difficult mother who so annoyed her fellow trustees that they left her to get on with things; her poor son eventually inherited an estate encumbered with £20,000 of debts.

Hugh, fourth Lord Clifford, determined to turn his fortunes around and by giving up his London house and generally economising, managed to put things in such good order that by 1760 he could contemplate completing the rebuilding of Ugbrooke. He it was who commissioned Robert Adam to prepare plans for a new house, and Capability Brown to landscape the grounds. Adam's plans were never fully implemented as Lord Clifford's

*Ugbrooke Park, c.1790, by Hendrik de Cot.*  Courtesy Lord Clifford

*Anne, 4th Lady Clifford.*
Courtesy Lord Clifford

*Charles, 6th Lord Clifford.*
Courtesy Lord Clifford

habits of economy prevailed almost to the end and only the library was finished according to Adam's drawings.  As freestanding Catholic churches were not permitted, the chapel had to be incorporated into the house and Adam planned the library wing to connect the new house,  thus disguising the chapel, also designed by Adam, but altered in the 1830s and enlarged in 1866.  This  truly remarkable creation is not only a family chapel but also the Catholic parish church.  To many visitors, and to the Cliffords, it is the true heart of Ugbrooke.

Lord Clifford had married Lady Anne Lee, co-heiress of the Earl of Lichfield, who descended from Charles II via Barbara Villiers, and thus the blood of most of the noble families of Europe was in her veins.  They had a remarkable family, two sons becoming the fifth and sixth lords.  Their third son, Robert, barred from serving in England, joined the French army as an officer in the Irish Jacobite army (Dillons' Regiment), only leaving when the French king was executed.  He deserted and returned to England with a large selection of French fortification and battle plans.  An attempt to have him made Adjutant General failed because of his religion, but he was placed in charge of civilian espionage during the Revolutionary and Napoleonic Wars, and also became a founder of the Royal Institution.

The fourth son, Thomas, also served overseas becoming Chamberlain to the Grand Duke of Mecklenburg-Schwerin, and marrying a baroness.  Of the fourth Lord Clifford's four daughters, one became a nun, one died young, and the other two also died unmarried, possibly  because of their religion.

The fifth Lord Clifford suffered from ill health and died, aged thirty-seven, in 1793 to be succeeded by his brother Charles.  During Charles's lifetime, the Catholic Emancipation Bill was finally steered through Parliament by the Duke of Wellington, a friend of the family, and at last a Clifford could again take his seat in the House of Lords.  It is hard for us today to imagine what an effect this had, but such was its importance that on Lord Clifford's return to Ugbrooke, he was greeted by his tenants and neighbours, and a crowd of well-wishers 1000 strong. They escorted him up the drive singing 'See the Conquering Hero Comes' as if he had won a major military victory, instead of a great moral one. Young ladies presented him with garlands and he was generally fêted. His son, Hugh, however, spent so much time fighting good causes and helping lame ducks that he nearly bankrupted the estate and was eventually persuaded to live abroad, leaving the running of the estate to the more capable hands of his son, Charles. Ugbrooke was let to various religious bodies whilst his father was abroad, generally for a pittance, but Charles, eighth Lord Clifford moved back in 1859 and restored the family fortunes sufficiently to leave all of his seven children £10,000 apiece on his death in 1880. He was succeeded by his son Lewis, the ninth baron. Charles had two remarkable brothers. William became the Catholic Bishop of Clifton, the first Catholic son of a nobleman to be made a bishop since the Reformation, and he was consecrated personally by the Pope. General Sir Henry Hugh Clifford served in the Army and his letters from the Crimea, carefully preserved, give a vivid account of the battles For his bravery at Inkerman he became one of the first recipients of the VC.

*Hugh, 7th Lord Clifford, by J. Ramsay.* Courtesy Lord Clifford

During the twentieth century the future of Ugbrooke Park has been in doubt on more than one occasion. The ninth Lord Clifford had died childless in 1916 and was succeeded by his brother, known as 'silly Willy', who had spent much of his life in Australia and New Zealand. He was an eccentric character, 'half mad, half genius', and dabbled in many fields, usually unsuccessfully, although in later life he became an authority on radiology, discovering Clifford's Colour Rays. He was also practical enough to build his own home in New Zealand, which he called Ugbrooke, and which still stands. Against his father's wishes, he married a sixteen-year-old beauty (descended from the Bassett family of North Devon) and had three sons, before they separated. It was only on the death of his brother that he came to England, but he never lived at Ugbrooke which was still firmly occupied by his brother's widow, the childless Mabel. It is said that she could not bear the sight of Willy's eldest son, Charles, who was sent to school in England and was the heir apparent, because she was so jealous, and he could only visit his uncle at Ugbrooke when she was away.

*Sir Henry Hugh Clifford VC, by Podesti.*

Courtesy Lord Clifford

Charles became the eleventh Lord Clifford in 1943. He was born in New Zealand, as were his brothers Lewis and Bede, and surely the thought of selling up and remaining in the country that had become their home and where there were already a large number of Clifford relations must have occurred to them. But after a brief naval career which included service during the First World War ending up as an internee in Holland, he returned to England when his father inherited. Because of William's total lack of business acumen, Lewis, the ninth Lord, had left what was not entailed direct to Charles. Poor Charles had to cope not only with finding the death duties payable on Lewis's death, but owing to poor advice this was repeated on his father's death twenty-seven years later. He found it necessary to sell off large chunks of the Clifford lands; the Cornish, Warwickshire and Buckinghamshire estates went, as well as more than half

*Mabel, wife of the 9th Lord Clifford, by H. Thaddeus.* Courtesy Lord Clifford

*Charles, 11th Lord Clifford*
Courtesy Lord Clifford

*Lewis, 12th Lord Clifford.*
Courtesy Lord Clifford

of the Somerset lands, and all of the Kingsteignton estate which had been in the family since 1483. When the ninth lord, Lewis, inherited in 1880, the total Clifford estate stood at 4416 acres in Devon, 1562 in Warwickshire, 896 in Somerset, 128 in Cornwall and 858 in Bucks, a total of 7860 acres, worth £9109 per annum. After the sales this was reduced to about 3500 acres.

Charles's first wife, whom he married in 1917, gave birth to their daughter a year later but died of Spanish influenza shortly afterwards, so his home-coming to Ugbrooke after the war was not the joyful affair it should have been. He moved into the dower house as Aunt Mabel was still in occupation, and remained so until her death in 1921. He immersed himself in running the estates and trying to salvage them from his father's neglect. Charles did not remarry until 1940, and had no further children. He had moved back to the dower house, Lawell, in 1936 where he lived until his death in 1962.

During the war, Ugbrooke was let rent free to an evacuated school from Kent, and later it was used as a hostel for disabled Polish servicemen, at an annual rent of £10. By the time they left in 1952 the house was in an extremely poor state, so bad that Lord Clifford, who seemed never to have cared very much for it, abandoned any hope and used the downstairs, including the Adam rooms, as a grain store, with the priceless paintings still on the walls!

That was when his nephew, Hugh, stepped in. In 1956, he learnt that Lord Clifford was planning to let Ugbrooke permanently to a convent. Hugh said that whatever rent was being offered, he would better by £5 and take on the place himself.

His father, Lewis, twelfth Lord Clifford, who inherited the title but not the estate in 1962, died two years later. Lewis never lived at Ugbrooke, pursuing a successful business career in Australia. Hugh, his only son, was also

*Hugh, 13th Lord Clifford, and Lady Clifford on the first day of opening to the public.*

born in Tasmania (in 1916) and was sent to England to school in 1928, otherwise he might well have remained in Australia, and the story of Ugbrooke would have have a very different ending. Only his commitment to Ugbrooke ensured the stability that saved the estate. The Army was Hugh's chosen career, and he was commissioned into the Devonshire Regiment in 1936. During the war he served in Cyprus, the Middle East, Syria and the Western Desert, was captured in 1942 and sent to a prison camp in Italy from which he escaped a year later and joined the Italian partisans. After the war he served in Palestine, Singapore, Hong Kong and Malaya, until 1950 when he resigned his commission and opted for a more peaceful life, farming in Australia. Seven years later he made that fateful visit to Ugbrooke and decided to return permanently with his wife, Katherine, daughter of Lord Fisher, sons Thomas and Rollo, and daughters Cecilia and Sarah. As well as fulfilling the usual county duties, he was appointed Commander of the TA Battalion and ADC to HM the Queen, for which he was awarded the OBE in 1962. He worked tirelessly to restore Ugbrooke and had he not stepped in, the house would almost certainly have fallen into such serious disrepair that demolition would probably have been its ultimate fate. As it is, the estate is on a sound footing, thanks to Lord Hugh's management which included voluntary exile to Guernsey in 1983, which he loathed. He missed the House of Lords, which he had previously attended on average three times a week, seeing it as an opportunity for putting forward other people's opinions, other people's concerns and getting a grip on problems. A trust was formed to ensure that death duties would never again threaten the entirety of what was left, and the decision as made to open Ugbrooke to the public.

Tom Clifford succeeded in 1988, but he, too, had been born abroad. His own children, Georgina (b.1983), Alexander Thomas Hugh (b.1985), and Edward George (b.1988), were the first to be born a Ugbrooke since the fifth lord in 1756, and for the first time for a very long time indeed, the house is once again a proper family home.

Like his father, the fourteenth Lord Clifford, Thomas, pursued a military career. He was commissioned into the lst Battalion Coldstream Guards in 1967, and served with them until 1975 when an horrific car accident almost finished him off and left him with severely impaired sight. During this time he served in Belize, Central Europe, Turkey, Norway, and Northern Ireland. It is quite obvious that his time in Ireland has left lasting scars when he talks of the loss of many friends and says he tries not to be bitter about this, and not to be bitter about 'the man who now serves as education minister' there. The government, he says, expects so much from the armed forces, and gives so little. Whenever there is a strike or a problem – call in the Army; foot and mouth crisis – call in the Army; problems abroad – call in the Army. Yet there is never enough money, never enough support and they are expected to perform miracles on nothing, and even stand trial should things go wrong.

Captain Clifford, as he then was, has taken part in two Queen's Birthday Parades. As ADC to the Chief of Defence Staff he went all over the world meeting people of different cultures which he found fascinating, and attending NATO meetings. He was in Berlin for four months before taking up his last appointment as Adjutant at the Guards depot. More recently Lord Clifford has involved himself in getting proper recognition and protection for maritime war graves and has gained quiet satisfaction that a UNESCO convention, including Russia, has given this recognition for the first time.

*Thomas, 14th Lord Clifford by the commemorative plaque in recognition of his parents' work in the restoration of Ugbrooke Park.*

One of the first things Lord Clifford did when he took over from his father was to radically alter the times of opening at Ugbrooke; his parents had first opened in 1980, for five days a week, but not the weekend. He chose the most popular days, and included Sunday, but left the family some time to themselves. The English Heritage grant for re-roofing obliged him to open anyway, but he says it would be enormously selfish not to open the doors to people who want to see this beautiful and unusual house which he considers part of England's heritage. There are many pitfalls to owning a house such as Ugbrooke Park, and the two prayers frequently uttered by current owners are that the roof will last out their lifetime, and that they should be spared dry rot. Lord Clifford has had to cope with both. The roof was found to be in very poor repair, and the rendering was falling off in great chunks. Without grant aid – Lord Clifford shrugs and says he does not know what would have happened, but even so there were battles of will and of good taste. For some reason it was suggested that the castellations on the towers should be removed, but he held out against this; what Lord Clifford did suggest with some force was that the strange tubular mouldings around the window frames and doorways, added by the ninth Lord Clifford, should be removed, returning the house to its original Adam appearance. English Heritage would not hear of it, because the listing applied to the house as it appeared at that time, so Ugbrooke was restored to its 1900 look and not to its more attractive eighteenth-century style. Despite this, the grant was 40 per cent and the estate had to find 60 per cent of a bill that hardly bears thinking about.

Two attacks of dry rot in the library and small library also made a large dent in the finances, and Lord Clifford is aware that it is still lurking, another problem for the future.

Everything that goes on at Ugbrooke Park comes under Lord Clifford's efficient control; he says that army training is perfect for organising and getting things done. The estate derives its income from farm tenancies, a landfill site, and large aggregate quarry. The house is also used for receptions and conventions, charitable fund-raising events, and he holds commercial shoots with house guests, which he always attends. One lasting legacy he will leave is his restoration of the grounds, landscaped by Capability Brown in the eighteenth century. The gales of 1987 and 1990 cut swathes through the tree belts which took years to remove and replanting was a massive operation. An avenue of limes and several clumps of oak have been replanted and one of his major goals has been achieved; the Brown lakes have been desilted, so that once again, Ugbrooke and its park look worthy of each other.

◇◇ ◆ ◇◇

# COURTENAY *of Powderham*

In a county rich in old families and distinguished pedigrees, the Courtenays stand out as the oldest and the most distinguished. Never mind the Conquest and Domesday, England was an unimportant, unattractive, barren island to the family that had its roots at Courtenay on the Isle de France, which Ashton de Courtenay fortified as early as 1010. His descendants have had a most fascinating and exciting history. Crusading was irresistable to the knights of valour of the time, and Joscelin de Courtenay took part in the First Crusade, ending up as Prince of Galilee in 1112, and Count of Edessa, where he ruled for thirty-six years, marrying a sister of the Prince of Antioch. He fought against Saladin and is supposed to have met his end from falling masonry at the Siege of Jerusalem in 1187. His son was captured by the Saracens and ransomed by his sister, the Princess of Sidon. Another descendant of Ashton, Elizabeth, married a son of the French King Louis VI, but despite their royal matches the family preferred to keep the name of Courtenay, and it was as Courtenays that her three sons ruled as emperors of Constantinople, ending with Baldwin II who was deposed in 1261 when the Byzantine Greeks finally recaptured Constantinople, and the rule of the Courtenays was over for good.

There are two versions as to how the Courtenays found their way to England. Renaud, grandson, or great-grandson of Ashton, accompanied Louis VII on the Second Crusade. On their return, they fell out to such an extent that Louis confiscated all the French lands of the Courtenays, so Renaud departed across the Channel to be welcomed by Henry II, who gave him lands in Oxford (Sutton Courtenay). Another version states that Renaud accompanied Eleanor of Aquitaine, bride of Henry II, and remained here. Both versions agree that Renaud, or his son, Sir Reginald, married Hawise, 'Lady of Okehampton' and became Baron of Okehampton and Governor of Exeter Castle. Okehampton was the most important manor in Devon in medieval times, holding 92 knight's fees. Reginald's son, Robert, made the next prestigious marriage to Mary, daughter of the sixth (de Redvers) Earl of Devon. Three generations later, Sir Hugh Courtenay (d.1340) succeeded to the de Redvers or Rivers estates in 1293, after the death of Isabel, Countess of Devon, which included the manor of Plympton, second in size to Okehampton. It was not until 1335 that he was awarded the title Earl of Devon. Isabel was the Countess of Devon and sister of Baldwin, the last Earl of Devon of the original creation. This made the Courtenays by far the most powerful family in the county.

The Courtenays throughout their long history have proved adept at contracting advantageous marriages. The son of Sir Hugh, known as the first earl, married Margaret de Bohun, granddaughter of King Edward I who brought with her as part of her dowry the estates of Powderham. From this time onwards, the Courtenays were centre stage, and honours and advancements were heaped upon them and their enormous family of 17 children. The eldest son, another Hugh, fought at Agincourt and at the Battle of Crécy, and was created an original Knight of the Garter in 1348. Brother William became Archbishop of Canterbury, and it was the sixth brother, Philip, who inherited Powderham from his mother. He fought in the Spanish Wars and served as King's Lieutenant in Ireland from 1382 to 1393, from whom the present earl is directly descended.

Tiverton Castle became the seat of the main branch and the family continued to prosper. The fourth earl was Lord High Steward of England under Henry V and Thomas, the fifth earl, by marrying Margaret Beaufort, daughter of the powerful Duke of Somerset, could claim kinship with royalty as she was the great-great-granddaughter of Edward III. But all was not to be plain sailing, and troubled times were ahead. The Wars of the Roses were disastrous for the main branch of the Courtenays, and their history for the next hundred years reads like a Shakespearean tragedy. Sir Thomas died peacefully in 1458, but three of his sons and a son-in-law met violent ends within the space of ten years. The eldest son, Thomas, sixth earl, was beheaded after the Battle of Towton, near York, in 1461; his brother Henry, was seventh earl for five years until he was attainted for treason and beheaded in 1466, and Sir John, the eighth earl, died at the Battle of Tewkesbury in 1471, having been restored to his honours by Henry VI. And so the senior line, which had seen so much adventure and survived so long, came to an abrupt and bloody end.

*Edward Courtenay, Earl of Devon.*
Devon & Exeter Institution

Fortune swung in favour of the family again in the time of Henry VII who created Sir Edward Courtenay, a descendant of the second son of the second earl and Margaret de Bohun, Earl of Devon, and restored him to the family estates after his victory at Bosworth. He distinguished himself by defending Exeter against Perkin Warbeck whom he subsequently defeated. But such was the turbulence of the times that fortune could never be guaranteed for long. Sir William, the next earl, had married Princess Katherine Plantagenet, daughter of Edward IV. This meant their children had the blood of the Yorkist kings and thus could have a claim to the throne, not always an advantage in such difficult times. Sir William found himself accused, attainted and imprisoned: another Courtenay in the Tower of London. For the next year he must have lived in fear of losing his head, until released by Henry VIII, and restored to favour. Henry Courtenay, the eldest son, who was a cousin of the king, was created Marquess of Exeter in 1525. However, he was foolish enough to be implicated in the Western Rebellion, for which he predictably lost his head on Tower Green in 1539. Royal blood could be a very mixed blessing; his only son Edward was imprisoned in the Tower at the age of twelve where he remained for fifteen lonely years. He must have found life bewildering when he was eventually released by Queen Mary Tudor, who created him Earl of Devon in 1553 (the third creation). One account states that she found this young man sufficiently attractive to have hinted at marriage, but no doubt his early experiences would have made him doubly cautious of such an honour. Another version states that he aspired to her. Whichever is true, nothing came of it, and Queen Mary married Philip of Spain. It is interesting to speculate as to what course history might have followed if a Courtenay had married Mary Tudor. However, instead of a glorious life as king consort, poor Edward was implicated in the Wyatt Rebellion and returned to the Tower. When he was released he decided to go abroad and died in Italy in 1556, supposedly poisoned. He was not yet thirty.

And thus both senior lines of the Courtenay family died out and the title of Earl of Devon was considered extinct.

Sir Philip Courtenay, son of the second earl, is accredited with being the creator of Powderham Castle as it stands today. He built for himself a 'fortified manor house' that was never designed to withstand a siege. Nevertheless it occupied a strategic position on the River Kenn as it flows into the tidal estuary of the Exe, on the opposite bank to Topsham.

The Courtenays continued at Powderham unobtrusively, marrying the daughters of noble families, extending and embellishing the castle, and keeping their heads well and truly below the parapet and firmly on their shoulders. Sir William Courtenay, who inherited in 1735, was raised to the peerage as Viscount Courtenay just ten days before his death in 1762.

He made remarkable changes to the interior of Powderham. Not only did he introduce some of the earliest decorative rococo plaster ceilings but he divided the original great hall and created what many people consider to be one of the finest staircase halls to be seen anywhere. The walls are painted a rich blue-green and are profusely covered with a riot of plasterwork of an incredible delicacy that until very recently survived untouched. It was redecorated in 1975, adhering as closely as possible to the original. His son, also William, the second viscount inherited aged nineteen, and immediately he came of age, continued work on the castle, putting in new windows, moving entrances and rebuilding one of the towers. He and his wife had a large family of eleven daughters and only one son, William, who inherited as third viscount in 1788, one year short of his majority, which could not be celebrated until after the period of mourning for his father had expired. When that day came, the festivities must have been the talk of the county. William hired a marquee tent at a cost of £769 ls l0d and gave a sumptuous party.

*Three children of the 1st Viscount Courtenay.*

Courtesy Lord Devon

Brought up with all those sisters, the third viscount had gentle tastes in music and art, and decided his contribution to Powderham would be a room large enough for musical gatherings and grand parties. A marquee was just not good enough. Not for him the local architects and workmen

*11th Earl of Devon, d.1888.*
Devon & Exeter Institution

*Charles, 14th Earl of Devon, d.1927.*

*Revd the Hon. Hugh Courtenay, 15th Earl of Devon, d.1935.*

who had previously been employed. He went straight to the top and employed James Wyatt, and the Prince Regent's cabinet-makers for the furniture. The room is a beautiful addition to Powderham and has been in continuous use as a music room ever since. It is considered that the central dome is responsible for the perfect acoustics, and the integral organ dates from 1769. The third viscount had an unfortunate friendship with William Beckford who was forced to flee the country in 1784 in circumstances similar to those which did for Oscar Wilde, and the viscount was later implicated. As a result he left precipitously to avoid arrest in 1810 and went to New York, moving to Paris in 1814, where he died, unmarried, twenty-five years later.

Under the circumstances, it is somewhat surprising that his attempt to reclaim the earldom was successful. It is assumed that his heir presumptive, William, a cousin and son of the Bishop of Exeter, and highly respected as High Steward of Oxford University and Clerk to the Houses of Parliament, was largely instrumental in this move. In 1831 the claim was allowed, thus reviving the Earldom of Devon after nearly three-hundred years.

It is fortunate that no one Courtenay was ever sufficiently wealthy to sweep away the work of his forebears and replace it with whatever was currently fashionable, so that some fine examples of all periods, except the very earliest, survive at Powderham. William, the new Lord Devon, employed a Devon architect, Charles Fowler, who changed the main entrance to the west-facing side of the castle. He added a castellated gatehouse and flanking towers, thus creating an entrance courtyard – described as 'formidably baronial', but completely in keeping with the period. His most important legacy was the banqueting hall, inserted between the two towers of the main building. This room is a fine example of Victorian splendour, and the proportions are admirable. His son, the eleventh earl, completed the room by adding the linenfold panelling and the magnificent fireplace as a memorial to his father based on one in the Bishop's Palace at Exeter built for Bishop Courtenay in 1485. A most interesting touch is the complete series of coats of arms incorporated into the panelling, beginning with the earliest arms of Athon and tracing the French line, which died out in the eighteenth century, on one side, and from Renaud, or Reginald down through the long descents to the eleventh earl on the other. No doubt the eleventh earl wanted to record his pedigree after his father had gone to all the trouble of establishing it. He married a daughter of Hugh, first Lord Fortescue and had one son, (Edward) Baldwin, who very nearly brought the history of Powderham to a sad end.

There still exists at Powderham a copy of the sales particulars that were drawn up in 1886 as being the only way of resolving the huge gambling debts that Baldwin had accumulated. Thankfully, his father found other ways out of his predicament, and Powderham was never put on the market. Baldwin succeeded two years later, but died in poverty in an attic in 1891, upon which the estate passed to his father's brother, Henry, rector of Powderham. Henry's son died before his father, but left a family of two

daughters, and three sons, all of whom succeeded in turn, the eldest dying unmarried in 1927, and his two younger brothers, both ordained, rectors of Powderham and Honiton respectively, both dying in 1935. Only the youngest was married and it was left to his family of seven to continue the line, and somehow find a way of paying off the enormous bill for death duties with three deaths in eight years. This task fell on the shoulders of Charles Courtenay, seventeenth Earl of Devon, a young man of nineteen when he succeeded.

Lord Devon had served with the Coldstream Guards until in 1939 he married Venetia, the divorced wife of the Earl of Cottenham. It was expected that he should resign his commission, which he duly did. The Second World War altered many things, not least the attitude to divorcees, and good officers were at a premium, so Lord Devon rejoined his old regiment. It was whilst they were stationed in Norfolk near the Sandringham estate, that King George VI issued an invitation to all officers to come for a day's shoot to keep the pheasants under control. Lord Devon and one or two others similarly placed were not included and the word went round that 'they were good enough to shoot his Majesty's enemies, but not his Majesty's game birds'. The king extended his invitation.

Powderham escaped requisitioning somehow but it was used by the Grenadier Guards during the war, and it was rumoured that one of the German High Command had his eye on the castle for his own residence once they had won. Later, in 1945, Lady Devon started a domestic science college to take the place of the finishing schools abroad and this lasted for some five years. Both the seventeenth earl and his wife were very involved in local life; he served on the District Council and County Council and was a strong supporter of the Church.

It was not an easy time for landowners with the agricultural slump and the present earl regards his father's considerable efforts with admiration and thinks it a miracle that so much of the estate has survived intact.

*The 18th Earl of Devon and his family in the Great Hall at Powderham.*
Courtesy Lord Devon.

The Earls of Devon and Powderham Castle are in fine fettle, and look set to continue running successfully for as far into the future as anyone can foresee. That is the opinion of Hugh Courtenay, eighteenth Earl of Devon, who has every right to survey his well maintained acres and thriving business with satisfaction. For that is what he has turned Powderham Castle into: a business, family-run, and essential for the continuance of Powderham Castle and the estate as a whole. No one part of the estate is more important than another and if Powderham is to survive, then all must pull together. But it is no longer possible for the castle to be supported by the land. Because of the crushing death duties his father had to find for two uncles who died in the same year, the acreage is much reduced. Large chunks of land in Newton Abbot, the Alphington estate on the outskirts of Exeter, the Walreddon estate in the Tavy Valley, the fishing rights on the Exe, and the Exeter canal were all sold, together with most of the village of Kenton, and the total acreage now stands at 3700. But Lord Devon takes an optimistic view of the future. Various changes in rules and regulations which mean that agricultural land is no longer liable for inheritance tax, make the possibility of passing everything down to the next generation much better than it used to be. The estate was placed in trust in 1965 to safeguard its future, but again, changes in the rules made it necessary to take it out again in 1985. Restrictive agricultural tenancies made it more attractive to farm 'in hand' using contract farmers, but here again things are changing so that it has been possible to return to the former methods.

Powderham was opened to the public for the first time in 1957. Although the family move back to a farmhouse during the summer months, Lord Devon enjoys sharing the castle and reckons it comes much more alive. His view is that tourism in the South West will need to move much more 'up market' as the 'bucket and spade brigade' tend to go abroad rather than to the beaches of South Devon and he is looking for an extended season, with many more foreign visitors. A relatively new venture, and one that is proving highly successful, is the opening of the shopping complex and popular restaurant at the entrance to the park and several times throughout the summer the parkland becomes the venue for open air concerts.

All these elements help towards the upkeep of the castle, and Lord Devon finds it gratifying that the estate has once again become a major employer in the locality, the central hub of the local economy although in a different fashion. It is important to him that Powderham represents some kind of stability and is of benefit to the area. It is also important, and part of his philosophy, that Lord Courtenay, Charlie his son and heir, is consulted on all major decisions. At present Lord Courtenay is a London-based barrister but he takes a keen interest in the estate, and there is no question of him not taking over when the times comes.

◇◇◆◇◇

# CRUWYS *of Cruwys Morchard*

## *Vigilate*

One of Devon's oldest families, one of those essentially English land-holders that have formed the backbone of the county, the Cruwys family still occupy their lovely, mellow manor house next door to the church of which they have held the patronage since at least 1262, when Robert de Crues presented the first recorded rector. Church and manor are inextricably linked; it is dedicated to the Holy Cross, and Cruwys is the celtic word for cross, and Morchard, the green wood.

The estate was held under a knight's fee from the Traceys, and the early Cruwys menfolk were knighted for their part in the battles in which they were required to give service, Sir Richard in King John's time, and Sir Robert in the days of Edward III. He was also noted for his valour at the Battle of Crécy. It was his predecessor, Sir Alexander, who is credited with the infamous encounter on Bickleigh Bridge when he met with a member

*Cruwys Morchard House.*

of the Carew family. Neither of them would give way to the other, and a fight ensued which ended with the Carew falling off the bridge to his death in the river below. One version states that the Cruwys had to forfeit 22 of their manors but, sad to relate, there is no evidence to support this story in the records of either family.

The Cruwys family is exceptionally well documented; from 1200 onwards all important papers have been stored away. There has never been a major fire at Morchard House, nor did the family deposit their records for safe-keeping with an Exeter solicitor, so that they have survived unscathed, largely because they were completely forgotten. The very earliest charters, from the twelfth century until 1552, were treated with great care for several centuries as they were required on more than once occasion to defeat a false claim to the estate. But the later documents lay undisturbed until 1926 when they were discovered in old boxes, tin trunks sandwiched between parts of a four-poster bed, butterfly specimen boxes, globes, pictures of family picnics, eighteenth-century waistcoats, medicine chests, wig stands and the usual discarded possessions of earlier generations to be found in a country house lumber room. Fortunately, the chatelaine of Morchard House was Mrs Margaret Cruwys, herself a historian, so that this remark-able find was in safe hands, and the documents were all listed and prop-erly stored, remaining to this day at Morchard House.

As early as 1241, Sir Alexander Cruwys of Cruwys Morchard, held East Anstey of Oliver Dinham. By the end of the century the family also had lands at Alfardisworthy in Bradworthy, Over Woolecomb at Mortehoe, and later still at Rackenford, all recorded and documented.

The most fascinating and colourful of the documents is the copy of the Calais Roll, an Elizabethan copy of the original which includes:

> ...the names and armes of the Principall captaines as well as Noblemen as of Knights that were with the victorious Kinge Edwarde the thirde at the asseige of Callis the twenteth year of his regne which was Anno Domni 1346...

...together with hand-painted shields, lists of wages, lists of north and south fleets and the ports from which they were supplied, and the lists of servants, domestic and otherwise, including Queen Philippa's butler – and 18 various musicians she brought along with her to provide entertainment after the battle's victorious conclusion. On his return, Sir Robert set about repairing some of the decline caused by his father, who had 'greatly exhausted and encumbered the estates', no doubt helped by his share of the spoils of Calais.

A century later, Thomas Cruwys was one of his many fellow countrymen to be on the wrong side at the Battle of Towton. The Cruwyses followed the lead of the Courtenays; unlike the earl, Thomas Cruwys kept his head but lost his lands. His Royal Pardon is still at Morchard House. He was not so lucky at Tewkesbury where he was either killed or executed. Thereafter the family contented themselves with their estates, staying firmly at home throughout the Civil War despite the Parliamentary leanings of Henry Cruwys and the call for him to bring his troops to the assistance of the people of Tiverton.

By this time the Cruwys's estates were at their zenith, with manors and holdings all over Devon, but with Humphrey (d.1621) and his son Lewis (d.1641) the family fortunes seemed to decline, for no apparent reason. Sales were held, and by 1637 some 20 holdings had gone. Lewis's son, Alexander, continued selling, including holdings in Cruwys Morchard itself. He had no children so the much diminished estates passed to his youngest brother Henry, as the middle brother, Matthew, had run away and was presumed dead. However, Henry had to fight off claims from a woman calling herself Sarah Cruwys, purporting to be Matthew's daughter, and Henry must have had doubts as he bought her off with £300 and a promise of another £300 should she outlive him. A few years later another supposed son of the lost Matthew appeared and this claim went as far as the Courts of Chancery, where it was dismissed. After Henry's death in 1667, and whilst his son, John, was still a minor, Sarah had another attempt at claiming the estates, but was unsuccessful.

*Sarah Foote.* Courtesy Cruwys family

The family fortunes were to some extent restored when John married Sarah Foote, one of the five heiresses of Samuel Foote MP for Tiverton. She brought with her £1500, but John after only three years recorded that his 'hasty and inconsiderate marriage was a very folly'. He used his wife's money as trading capital in the serge business, collaborating with his brother-in-law, Robert Burridge of Tiverton, a considerable merchant of the time. He also dealt in grain, supplying the Victualling Office at Plymouth, and in 1690 was appointed Receiver General for Poll Tax in Devon. He died of smallpox in 1711. John and Sarah's son, Samuel Cruwys, was the first of the family to seek a career and to leave his home county behind him. He trained in London as a barrister and, with most of his time being spent in the capital, in 1713 married Susanna Bretton, daughter of a London vintner.

Samuel left the running of his country estates to his younger brothers and sisters, although two of his brothers later joined him in his successful legal practice. He became a Fellow of the Royal Society, and was appointed solicitor to the Stamp Office, a lucrative position that he passed to his nephew Thomas on his retirement in 1749. His legal mind was brought to bear on a long-running dispute over the churchyard at Cruwys Morchard. The family chapel had been destroyed by Cromwell's men:

*John Cruwys.* Courtesy Cruwys family

*I will certainly sett a mark on the Bounds of it and am determined to Separate my own Isle to my own use as other Patrons do, or else the Parish will claim this from me hereafter…*

A line of fir trees was planted and…

*…within these trees is in the Inheritance of the Cruwys's and is no part of the church yard…the isle in the church is separated by a long mortar moulding in the roof in a line with the chancel.'*

*Revd Henry Shortrudge Cruwys.*
Courtesy Cruwys family

*George Sharland Cruwys.*
Courtesy Cruwys family

*George James Cruwys and Mary Owen.*
Courtesy Cruwys family

Perhaps he foresaw problems, as his only son John became rector of Cruwys Morchard in 1741 when he was twenty-five, and lived there for the rest of his life as both squire and parson. He died a bachelor fifty years later, and was succeeded by his nephew, the Revd Henry Shortrudge Cruwys, whose father had married the daughter of the town clerk of South Molton. He had seven children, but only three survived infancy and there is a sad story that his only son died at the age of fifteen as a result of bullying at school. With Dr Cruwys's death in 1804, the male descent of the family came to an end after over five-hundred years.

Amongst the doctor's papers is an early example of self-assessment made when income tax was introduced in 1799, before all income and property was taxed 'at source'. The income of the estate is given as £595 18s 8d, with rent from holdings accounting for £283 10s 5d, and the Glebe and Tithe, £263 8s 3d. The deductions amount to nearly £300, including £100 apiece for his two sons-in-law, £36 8s for the poor and church rate, 19 guineas and £13 on land tax for Morchard House and the parsonage respectively, and smaller sums for repairs to the house and other properties – incurring an Income Act Duty of £30 1s 6d.

To Harriet, the elder of the two surviving daughters, passed the Cruwys Morchard estate. She had married George Sharland, described as a money scrivener, of South Molton in 1794, and already had five children when they moved to Morchard House, where a further four were born, so for the first time for a long time, the large house would have echoed to the sounds of children's voices and the rooms come to life as they romped all over it. The Sharlands were a well-established South Molton family, prospering as clothiers and weavers, becoming yeomen and owning Fort House, 'The Sign of the George' in the town, and Parke House at Bishop's Nympton, where they lived. Six years after their marriage, George Sharland was virtually bankrupt, and was put out of office 'because he hath committed a wilfull and corrupt perjury'. Sales of most of the Sharland property followed in 1806, including Parke House, Fort House and much of the land.

George and Harriet's eldest surviving son, also George, added Cruwys to his name and followed his grandfather to the family living, becoming the third 'squarson' to live at Cruwys Morchard Court, as the house was then known. His bride was Mary Riddell, daughter of a wealthy Tiverton man, and was said to have a hogshead of gold. Whether it was with her money or his, George Sharland Cruwys is reputed to have spent over £1000 on repairs, flooring the hall with new boards and erecting a staircase, all of which came from Enmore Castle in Somerset. He also set about bringing the dilapidated house up to date, although later generations might wish he had not removed the 'quaint old fireplaces and antiquated panelling'. The couple kept their own pack of hounds and no doubt entertained the local families, although George complained of lack of income, having also inherited a debt of £1500 when his father died in 1831. He had to sell more property to educate his sons, and complained that his only extravagance was to take a first-class rail ticket when he could have made do with a second-class. However, when his wife Mary died in 1871, she left the considerable sum of £15,048 to be divided between their two sons. Three years later, George Sharland Cruwys also died and James Cruwys succeeded. Life for him and his wife, Mary Owen, was fairly typical, revolving around the annual cycle of hunting, shooting, cricket in the summer, serving as a JP and keeping the estate and parish in good order. He was also a keen gardener and was responsible for many of the fine trees around the house and parkland. He died in 1904.

*Lewis Cruwys.*

Lewis, his eldest son, was a professional soldier, and it was his wife, Margaret, who discovered the treasure trove of documents. As they had no children, the estate passed to his brother, the Reverend Jeffrey Cruwys whom he (Lewis) had appointed rector in 1916 and who remained in that post until 1950. Jeffrey Cruwys surrendered his right to inherit the estate, but died before his elder brother so that the present Squire Cruwys inherited from his Uncle Lewis who held the estate from 1904 to 1957. During these fifty-three years, Lewis Cruwys had not increased the rents of any of his tenants so it fell to his heir, Edgar Cruwys, to do so and repair the dilap-

*Edgar and Mary Cruwys, with their son Guy and his wife Sarah.*

idated farms and mansion house, none of which had modern plumbing, drains, electricty, bathrooms, hot and cold piped water supply, or cooking facilities.

He was still serving in the Royal Air Force (1938–1963) but he and his wife Mary started at once on the task of making the manor house habitable and the farms viable. They put in hand the repairing of leaking roofs, the bringing in of piped water supplies and electricity and providing drains and replacing Victorian cooking arrangements. They finally moved into the manor house on returning from the RAF in 1963, with their two children Caroline (b.1943), and Guy (b.1946). Guy followed the family tradition of studying for the Law, but before he and his new wife Sarah had time to settle down to life in London, in 1974, his father announced his intention of handing over to the next generation. Guy and Sarah moved into Cruwys Morchard House in time for the birth of their first child. They have lived there since then with their four children, Emily, Robert, Mary and Belinda. Edgar and Mary Cruwys have moved into the Old Rectory which is where Edgar was born.

# FANE TREFUSIS

## *Tout vient de Dieu* – Everything comes from God

Whilst the Clinton barony is, without doubt, one of the oldest in the country, its first connection with Devon was not until the middle of the seventeenth century when Lady Arabella Clinton, younger daughter of the twelfth Baron Clinton, married Robert Rolle of Heanton Satchville. Through two of their three children, Samuel and Bridget, and Arabella's sister, Margaret, the barony descended in turn, down to the present baron.

For most of their long history, the Clintons have been involved in affairs of state, playing an important role, and every generation seems to have made its mark, beginning with the first baron, John de Clinton, who served Edward I in the Scottish and French campaigns. He was born around 1258, and through his wife, settled at the manor of Maxstoke in Warwickshire, which remained the family's main home until the fifth baron exchanged it for lands in Northamptonshire. From the beginning it seems there was doubt as to whether the title was hereditary and the issue became more confused as at one stage when, following the death of their father in 1310, both of the first baron's sons were known as Lord Clinton. However, the younger brother was created Earl of Huntingdon and his elder brother, John, became the second Baron Clinton. But what did become apparent was that the original creation was to 'heirs general', meaning that it could pass through the female line, a most unusual provision.

The ninth baron, Edward, who succeeded as a boy of five in 1517, held the post of Lord High Admiral under Edward VI from 1550 until his death in 1585, with one interruption of five years during Queen Mary's reign. He first married first Elizabeth Blount, a former mistress of Henry VIII and mother of his son, Henry Fitzroy, Duke of Richmond. She brought with her an estate in Lincolnshire and for the rest of his life Edward played a prominent part in the affairs of that county. In 1572, Queen Elizabeth rewarded her faithful servant with the earldom of Lincoln 'for his services to Henry VIII, Edward VI, and Queen Mary, and to the present Queen

Elizabeth, particularly during the late rebellion in the north, and for his service as High Admiral'. It was from his third wife, Elizabeth, grand-daughter of the Marquess of Dorset, that the barony descended via their son Henry.

Theophilus, the twelfth baron and fourth Earl of Lincoln (b.1600), led an adventurous life. He raised an army of 300 volunteers to fight during the Thirty Years War on the side of the Elector Palatine, Charles I's brother-in-law, but was imprisoned in the Tower when he opposed that monarch's proposed forced loan. He became a Parliamentarian, commanding a regiment, and was appointed Speaker of the House of Lords in 1647. At the Restoration he became Commissioner for the Colonies.

Edward, his grandson, fifth earl and thirteenth baron, died childless in 1692. As the earldom of Lincoln could not pass through the female line, it passed to a cousin. The barony of Clinton fell into abeyance between the surviving descendants of Theophilus. Catherine, his eldest daughter, had one son, Vere Booth, who died unmarried in 1717, and with him any claim to the barony.

Arabella and Margaret, his two younger daughters, both made advantageous marriages that had great impact not only on their own family but also on the county. Arabella married Robert Rolle of Heanton Satchville in Devon. Her sister married Hugh Boscawen, a prominent Cornish landowner of Tregothnan, whose descendants are now Lords Falmouth, still at Tregothnan. Hugh's mother was also a Rolle, Margaret, the sister of Sir Samuel, so the family links with this prestigious Devon family were close.

Margaret Boscawen had one daughter, Bridget, who married Hugh Fortescue of Filleigh and they had a daughter, Margaret, and four sons, of

*An early drawing of Heanton Satchville is all that survives of a magnificent house.*

whom only Hugh survived. This Hugh successfully claimed the barony, becoming the fourteenth baron in 1721. He was also created Baron Fortescue of Castle Hill, and the first and last Earl Clinton, as this title expired when he died unmarried in 1751. His sister Margaret styled herself Baroness Clinton after her brother's death.

Arabella and Robert Rolle had one son, Samuel, and a daughter, Bridget. As Samuel died in 1719 his daughter Margaret, aged only ten, became heir to the title. At the age of fifteen she was married to Robert Walpole, later the Earl of Orford, son of Sir Robert, the Prime Minister, and builder of Houghton Hall in Norfolk. It was a far from happy marriage, but they did produce one son, George, before Margaret left Lord Orford, and spent most of the rest of her life on the Continent, virtually in exile because of her scandalous conduct with a succession of lovers. She did return to England on the death of her husband, and remarried, but this, too, did not last and she went back to her Italian life and lovers, dying in Pisa, where she was buried in 1781.

George Walpole, their son, became the sixteenth Baron Clinton and third Earl of Orford. Despite the wealth of his father and grandfather, all poor George was left with was an enormous burden of debts estimated at around £40,000, and a huge house. When he died unmarried in 1791, the barony was claimed by his cousin, Robert George William Trefusis, great-great-grandson of Bridget Rolle, Samuel Rolle's sister, who had married Francis Trefusis of Trefusis in Cornwall, which is still the family's home. Under the terms of Samuel Rolle's will, George Orford could have terminated the entail of the Rolle estate, which he never visited, so that it would have passed to the Walpole family. But he did not, so the Rolle estates in Devon and Cornwall passed to the Trefusis family although by now they were heavily encumbered with mortgages, an unwanted legacy from the Walpoles. It took two years for Robert Trefusis's claim to be granted. Finally in February 1794, he was summoned to Parliament as the seventeenth Baron Clinton.

## THE ROLLE FAMILY

The Rolle family dominated Devon from the mid-sixteenth century until the end of the nineteenth, and at one time their land holdings were vast. Their oldest manor appears to have been Stevenstone, outside Torrington, where George Rolle died in 1552. He was a prosperous London merchant who added considerably to his holdings by purchasing former monastic lands and manors. He had three wives and an enormous family of 20 children, and from three of his sons descended the several branches of Rolle – one of his sons, Henry is commemorated in Petrockstowe church with 18 of his own children. But this is another ancient family name that has disappeared.

From John, the eldest son, descended Sir Henry Rolle of Stevenstone, who died in 1625 and was buried at St Giles in the Wood. His son, also Henry, made a prestigious marriage to Anne, daughter and co-heir of Thomas

My Children feare the lorde

*Brasses in Petrockstowe church of Henry Rolle and his wife Margaret and their numerous children. Now divided into two, the brasses are likely to have been one, the division being in the centre of the Rolle shield.*

Dennys of Bicton and Holcombe, and it was their son, Dennys Rolle who, at the age of eleven, succeeded his grandfather, and to his mother's East Devon estates. When he died in 1638 he was the first Rolle to be buried at Bicton. As his own son had died in infancy, Dennys's successor was his cousin Henry of Beam, near Torrington.

Robert Rolle of Heanton, who married Lady Arabella Clinton, was MP for Devon in 1654 and 1658, and for Callington in 1660. His brother began the line that lived at Hudscott, also near Torrington and whose family provided a succession of MPs, all sitting for Callington, the family seat.

John Rolle (b.1756) succeeded to the estates of his Uncle Henry, who had been created Baron Rolle of Stevenstone in 1748. His father Dennys, had inherited two other portions of the Rolle estates and was said to have an annual rent roll of some £40,000 per annum, so that on his death in 1797, John Rolle was in possession of the entire Rolle estate. He represented Devon in Parliament, was a Colonel of the North Devon Militia, and was created Baron Rolle of Stevenstone in 1796. His second wife was the Hon. Louisa Trefusis, daughter of Robert, seventeenth Lord Clinton. He had no children so that with him the Rolle family in the male line died out.

Robert, seventeenth Baron Clinton, and his Swiss wife, Albertina, moved into Heanton House once their claim was successful, but only three years later it burnt down. Both Robert and his wife died tragically young, Robert in 1797 aged only thirty-three and a year later his wife, leaving a child of ten to succeed as eighteenth baron, the fifth holder in one century. As soon as young Robert came of age, he purchased a house called Huish, a short distance away, which was re-named Heanton Satchville. After the upheavals of the previous century, the family must have looked forward to

*Lord John Rolle in his coronation robes.*

*Huish, re-named Heanton Satchville.*

a period of calm, but a new threat was posed when Lord Cholmondely, heir to the Walpole estates, made a claim on the Rolle lands. This took nine years of no-doubt expensive legal wrangling to resolve finally in favour of the Clintons.

For Robert these must have been busy years. Not only was he coping with the claim, and re-establishing his seat, with the responsibility for his siblings, but he was a professional soldier serving as ADC to the Duke of Wellington in the Peninsular War, in 1812 carrying the despatches from the Battle of Salamanca to Downing Street and to the Prince Regent. He married twice, his second wife being Francis, daughter of William Poyntz of Cowdray Park. This gave the family their connection with the Spencers as her sister Elizabeth had married the fourth Earl Spencer, who was also her second cousin. Robert died without issue in Italy in 1832, aged forty-five. His brother, Charles Rodolph became the nineteenth baron a year after his marriage to Lady Elizabeth Kerr, the daughter of the Marquess of Lothian, and a granddaughter of the Duke of Buccleuch.

Of the rest of Robert and Albertina's children, George the third son, followed a naval career and, of his descendants, one became Bishop of Crediton, two were killed in the First World War, and Louisa, the youngest daughter, married in 1822, John, Lord Rolle.

The nineteenth baron studied at Oriel College Oxford where he gained an MA in 1817, becoming a Fellow of All Souls and a member of Lincoln's Inn. Much of his time must have been spent keeping the estates, still heavily mortgaged, in order and finding sufficient funds to pay the numerous jointures and allowances and mortgages with which it was heavily encumbered, which included an annual payment of £1000 to the widow of the eighteenth baron, and a similar sum to his own mother. It would seem that marriage settlements involved the promise of annual payments, whether an estate could afford them or not, and often the only way out was a mortgage.

*Bicton House, c.1830.*

Charles Henry Rolle Trefusis, the eldest son of a family of eight, was born in Rome in 1834. He was intelligent and well-educated, with a serious mind and a High Church faith. Whilst a young man he fell in love with Harriet Forbes, and had to overcome strong family opposition for they were first cousins, their mothers being the daughters of William Kerr, Marquess of Lothian. Finances were again a major problem. His father was…

*…living principally upon allowances granted to me by the Court of Chancery for the upkeep of Stevenstone and for my brother Mark, and upon money borrowed from a Torrington bank for the upkeep of my large family.*

He did not see how he could provide for the young couple, and expected help from Harriet's family, which was not forthcoming. The couple had to keep their engagement of 1856 a secret. By 1858 the two families reached an agreement whereby Lord Clinton guaranteed them £700 per annum for life, with an additional £300 when the Dowager Lady Clinton died, and his brother Mark guaranteed Harriet £1000 from the Rolle estates should Charles predecease her. They were married at Fasque, close to Harriet's home of Fettercairn in Scotland.

*Mark Rolle.*
Gt Torrington Town Lands, Alms Lands and Poors Charity & Torrington Museum

The couple made a triumphant return to Heanton, being met at the station by a military escort which led them to Dolton village, where the bells were ringing and the flags flying, and all the people were cheering. After lunch, the couple were escorted through floral arches and past the local band to Heanton House, which was also decorated and with all the tenants and servants up on the roof. A marquee had been erected for the 300 wedding guests, along with a tent for 300 tenants and estate workers, with a second dinner the following day for all those who had had to work the first! Dancing followed after dinner, which lasted until 5am. Married life began at Heanton as there was no question of the young couple being able to afford their own home to begin with, and it would seem they had some difficulty steering a course between Lord Clinton and Aunt Louisa at Bicton, who was quite demanding, but generous in her support.

Charles, who had won the North Devon seat in 1857, remained active in Parliament. In 1866 he succeeded as the twentieth baron, and the following year Harriet succeeded to her father's estates of Fettercairn and Pitsligo, so the couple's financial worries must at last have seemed behind them, despite the mortgages and jointures. Lord Clinton's estates amounted to 18,135 acres in England (14,431 in Devon) valued at £23,246 per annum, and 16,655 in Scotland with an annual value of £14,230, a far cry from £700 per year. By now the couple had five children, and Charles, in accordance with his father-in-law's will, took the additional names of Hepburn-Stuart-Forbes. But their happiness was short-lived. In 1869 Harriet died. Lord Clinton was devastated and gave up public and political life. Six years later, he married Margaret, daughter of Sir John Walrond from Uffculme (and had a further seven children), and returned to public life as a Charity Commissioner. He was appointed Lord Lieutenant in 1887, a position he held until his death in 1904. Since 1863 he had been Chairman of the Devon Quarter Sessions, the old established method of running the county, which was to change in 1888 with the formation of the County Council. Lord Clinton took an active part in electioneering, was duly elected, and served as Chairman of the new council until 1903 when he resigned on health grounds. His last duty was at the reception given to General Sir Redvers Buller on his return from the South African campaign when he presented him with a sword of honour.

*Charles, 20th Baron Clinton.*
Devon County Council

For the sake of his health, Lord Clinton travelled to Egypt that winter, accompanied by a doctor and nurse, but died in Cairo, aged seventy in 1904. His body was brought back to England, travelling from Waterloo to Okehampton by train on 3 May. He was laid to rest in Huish church which he had rebuilt in memory of his beloved Harriet.

Mark George Kerr Trefusis was the second son of the nineteenth baron. His Aunt Louisa had married Lord John Rolle, who decided to make Mark his heir should he die without children, as seemed likely. In 1797, Lord Rolle had succeeded to his father's estates centred on Bicton in East Devon and Stevenstone near Torrington. Following the death of his first wife, he married in 1822, Louisa, daughter of the seventeenth Baron Clinton, then aged twenty-four; he was seventy, and there were no children. On his death at the age of ninety-two in 1842, young Mark, aged six, inherited these vast estates of over 55,000 acres, two large houses and an assured annual income vastly in excess of his brother's. In accordance with the terms of the will, Mark changed his name to Rolle, and when he came of age moved to Stevenstone. Aunt Louisa had the use of Bicton, and the London house for her life together with an annuity of £10,000, which gave her considerable power within family circles.

*Louisa, Lady Rolle, in her robes for the coronation of Queen Victoria.*
Gt Torrington Town Lands, Alms Lands
and Poors Charity & Torrington Museum

Charles Henry, the twentieth Baron Clinton, was concerned for his large family. Had he survived his brother Mark, the Rolle estates would have passed to him and he proposed to divide them between his younger children, with Charles, his heir, inheriting the Devon Clinton estates and Harry, the second son, the Cornish estates. But he could not break the entail of the Rolle estates whilst his brother was alive, and Mark survived him by three years.

In the event both estates passed to his eldest son, Charles John Robert Hepburn-Stuart-Forbes-Trefusis, twenty-first baron, who had already inherited his mother's Scottish estates on her death, and it was at Fettercairn that he and his bride, Lady Jane Grey McDonnell, a distant cousin, made their home. He made a bid for a Scottish seat, and on losing, entered into local political life. Their two daughters, Harriet and Fenella, were both born at Fettercairn, and were young ladies by the time their grandfather died and the family moved south to Heanton. Within a year, the twenty-first Baron Clinton had been made an alderman and JP. Three years later he also inherited the Rolle estates from his Uncle Mark. By now he was a man of considerable property and influence and was appointed to the Council of the Duchy of Cornwall and Keeper of the Privy Seal to the Prince of Wales, holding both positions until 1933. He was an active member of the House of Lords, especially in all matters to do with agriculture, forestry, and land.

A keen and knowledgeable supporter of Forestry, Lord Clinton was appointed to the Interim Forestry Authority set up in 1918 to make good the losses of woodland and the development of afforestation. This was the forerunner of the Forestry Commission, with which both he and his successor have been involved. Lord Clinton was one of the eight original commissioners with powers to create forests to serve the nation's needs in a future emergency. The objective was to acquire and plant 1,770,000 acres, a formidable task. After the first meeting of the Commission, Lord Clinton stole a neat march on his Chairman, Lord Lovat. It had been agreed that the two would have a race to see who could plant the first trees. Lord Clinton telegraphed ahead, and when he arrived at Eggesford Station, he was met by his men equipped with spades all ready to plant the seedlings. The task accomplished, Lord Clinton sent a telegram to greet Lord Lovat

*21st Baron Clinton.*

*The occasion of the Golden Wedding of the 21st Baron Clinton and his wife at Bicton. June 1936. Charles Fane is seated on the steps with his wife Gladys and their son Gerard, the present Lord Clinton.*

when he arrived at Elgin. Those trees still survive in the Forestry Commission woods at Eggesford.

For ten years from 1919, Lord Clinton was Chairman of the Forestry Commission, supplying from his own nurseries an annual total of some 100,000 seedlings and it is in no small measure due to his leadership that the Commission was successful beyond expectation in those early years. Lord Clinton foresaw the approaching agricultural disaster as the landowner was being squeezed on both sides, with nothing left to help tenants out in a crisis. He campaigned for a reduction in the rate of death duties on land as unfair when compared to taxation on other assets, and also detrimental to farming, 'threatening the extinction of the agricultural owner as a class'.

The twenty-first Baron Clinton was made Lord Warden of the Stannaries of Cornwall and Devon in 1921, and a Privy Councillor in 1926. On his retirement from public life, George V made him a Knight Grand Cross of the Victorian Order. His retirement was marred when, on 18 December 1932, Heanton House burnt down for the second time and had to be rebuilt, this time to designs by Walter Tapper.

*The marriage of Charles Fane and Gladys Lowther, from* The Times *1933.*

When he died in 1957, memorial services were held simultaneously with the burial service at Huish, at Exeter Cathedral, Torrington and several East Devon churches to mark the passing of a man who had held sway over the largest estate Devon had ever seen.

The barony fell into abeyance between the twenty-first baron's two daughters. Harriet, the elder married Major Henry Fane, and their eldest son Charles was killed in the Second World War, leaving a son, Gerard, aged six. Fenella married the Hon. John Bowes-Lyon, a brother of the Queen Mother, but had only daughters. A year after his grandmother Harriet died, Gerard Neville Mark Fane claimed the barony, his Great-Aunt Fenella waiving her claim in his favour. In 1965, he was successful and took the additional surname of Trefusis, becoming the twenty-second baron.

ELIZABETH ANSON'S
GRAND PARENTS.

Lord Clinton will tell you that he was brought up all over the country; his father was killed in the war and his stepfather was also a soldier, but he was a frequent visitor to Heanton and to Bicton, and remembers his great-grandfather, the twenty-first baron, and his wife Jenny. He remembers that calmer world when Lord Clinton had time to drive around the estate, talking to his tenants and spending time getting to know them; it was the way things had always been done. His successor finds things different, and not necessarily better. Thirty years ago he employed many more people than he does now, most of the work being contracted out. Farming then was divided between tenant farmers, and farming in-hand with perhaps an agent. Lord Clinton has six let farms and a Home Farm on the Heanton estate, and 1200 acres farmed 'in share', an Australian idea that seems similar to a concession. Forestry plays an important part in Lord Clinton's life and he has been appointed President of the Royal Forestry Association for a two year period. Until the reform of the House of Lords, he spoke with great knowledge on such matters, and anything affecting agriculture and land, as had his forebears. In common with most of his fellow peers, he deprecates the passing of a body of men with immense knowledge and disinterested experience behind them, prepared to give freely of their expertise and time.

He sees his role very much as custodian, preserving and ensuring that it is passed on to the next generation in good order. Lord Clinton considers that maintaining the large estates is essential to preserving the countryside, for without them things would quickly degenerate. Already he notices changes. Deer are proliferating where he has never seen deer before, and the grey squirrels are wreaking havoc with the woodland, posing a very real threat to the future of forestry. He sees also that a traditional estate such as Heanton should provide employment, and has been able to do this, both in forestry and in its sawmills. These enterprises provide many direct and indirect jobs, and contribute to the rural economy.

Some twenty years ago he got together with other Devon landowners with fishing interests when he realised that things were seriously wrong with the waters of the River Torridge (of which he owns some of the most beautiful stretches), and the Taw. Together, and he stresses he was only the initial force, they have brought pressure to bear upon the appropriate authorities to ensure a considerable improvement, and have through this amalgamation formulated and discussed plans, which have improved the general environment of these rivers. At the same time they formed the South West Rivers Trust, which is doing major works both in Devon and Cornwall with money allocated partly from Europe. In 2002 he feels it is time for him to step down.

Lord Clinton has been in a position to monitor some of the profound changes that have occurred since he inherited; there are fewer people on the land, fewer people employed directly, although a great number do still work, but under contract, and for other landowners as well. Farming is no longer 'a way of life' but a hard business where every part has to prove its value. Uneconomic parts are sold off without sentiment, such as thatched cottages which represent more of a liability to a landowner; smaller farms are amalgamated. There are far more people moving into the area, and taking an interest in how things are run, so that he feels he no longer needs to be the figurehead as was once expected. However, he feels that it is up to him to provide some continuity in such a beautiful area. Both of the two great estates around Heanton and Bicton – Stevenstone was sold off in the 1900s and in 1957 – are run along professional lines. A feature of both are the fine tracts of woodland, and specimen trees, planted by the twenty-first baron and the present Lord Clinton.

Lord Clinton married in 1959 Nicola Purdon Coote, who as well as serving as High Sheriff, and on numerous committees, has been appointed president of the Devon County Show for 2002. They lead a private family life, with their son, Charles, who takes a great interest in the estate and lives close to Bicton, their two daughters, and numerous grandchildren.

# FORTESCUE
## *of Castle Hill, Filleigh*

*Forte sutum salus ducum* – A strong shield is the safety of leaders

This remarkable family, which at one time had representatives in 46 Devon parishes and 20 elsewhere in the country, has produced a saint, a Lord Chief Justice whose work still forms the basis of English law, several notable soldiers, an eminent historian who chronicled the history of the British Army, and numerous politicians and courtiers of note. Throughout history, members of the family have quietly distinguished themselves, many in the military field, several as courtiers and servants of the Crown, as justices, sheriffs, and magistrates – unpaid and often arduous duties requiring long hours of travel in the days of horseback or in carriages over poor roads.

*Castle Hill.*

From the fifteenth century onwards the Fortescues have held lands in North Devon, centred on their principal seat at Castle Hill.

Their origins were in Normandy and it is a family tradition that Richard, known as le Fort – the Strong – saved King William's life no fewer than three times at Hastings by protecting him with his shield; from this stems both the family name and motto. He was rewarded with lands in South Devon. Hoskins, in *Devon* states that:

> *Whympstone is the oldest known home of the Fortescues....said to have been granted to them by King John in 1209, but they were in this district c.1140 when Ralph Fortescue gave lands to Modbury Priory at, or soon after its foundation. Nothing remains of their ancient house and the estate now belongs to the Plymouth Co-operative Society.*

Of the two sons of that early warrior, the younger, as a Knight of St John, accompanied Richard I on his crusades, and the elder remained at home, commanding a local army raised to quell rebellion against King John. The next member of the family to distinguish himself was Sir John, who fought at Agincourt and in 1422 was created Governor of the province of la Brie in France. By now the family had lands at Wimston, Preston and Spriddlestone, and Sir John's wife brought further estates at Norries and Sharpham. Their two remarkable sons rose to great heights in the legal world. Henry, the elder, represented the county in Parliament in 1421, and was sent to Ireland as Chief Justice of the Common Pleas. The younger brother John became the Lord Chief Justice of England in 1442, an office he held for eighteen years. It is his book *De Laudibus Legum Anglice* that forms the basis of English Common Law by which we are still governed. A loyal man, he backed Henry VI and the Lancastrians and when that monarch was dethroned in 1461, Sir John, at the age of seventy, fought for him at Towton, and escaped following the Lancastrian defeat. He followed the queen into exile, returning the following year for the final Battle of Tewkesbury where Sir John was taken prisoner. He suffered a kinder fate than many of his contemporaries, for Edward IV pardoned him and restored him to his position as Privy Councillor. This courageous man retired to the estate he had purchased at Ebrington in Gloucestershire, home of the present Earl Fortescue, and where he died, aged ninety, in 1486. From him are descended the major branches of the Fortescue family. It was a descendant, Sir Adrian of Punsborne in Oxfordshire, who having served Henry VIII in France, was later beheaded by that same monarch for refusing to acknowledge his Supremacy, and was later beatified as a martyr to the Roman Catholic faith.

*Brass in Filleigh church of Sir Richard, d.1570.*

His son served as Chancellor of the Exchequer to both Elizabeth I and James I. And another member of the family, George Fortescue of Filleigh, sailed round the world with Drake and died in command of the barque *Bonner* in the 1587 Carthagena expedition.

It was as a result of the Black Assizes of 1586 that John Fortescue of Wood acting as magistrate, lost his life through gaol fever. So many Spanish prisoners had been crammed into Exeter gaol by the victorious fleet, and whilst awaiting their ransom were so poorly fed and housed, that disease was rife, spreading rapidly to all in contact with the gaol. Several prominent families lost members through this cause.

The Fortescues have supplied numerous sheriffs, another unpaid honour, and numerous MPs from 1382 until the present day, and three have served as Lord Lieutenant. In the Parliament of 1592 there was a total of eight Fortescue Members from various constituencies all over the country.

The de Filleigh family go back to at least the fourteenth century when they were granted lands in the parish of East Buckland, Bray and Charles, all adjoining Filleigh. It was from this family that the lands eventually came to Elizabeth Densyll, and thus to the Fortescues when in 1454 she married Martin, son of Sir John, the Lord Chief Justice. For several generations the Fortescues stayed out of the public eye, taking no noticeable part in the Civil War and thus preserving their estates, and making judicious marriages, to a Chichester, and in 1612 to Mary Rolle of Heanton Satchville. Her grandson, Hugh, married his cousin Bridget, daughter and heiress of Hugh Boscawen and his wife, Lady Margaret Clinton (Rolle), and it was through her that Hugh's son, also Hugh, became the fourteenth baron Clinton in 1720. He had entered Parliament, and in 1721 was also appointed Lord Lieutenant of Devon. A post as Gentleman of the Bedchamber to the Prince of Wales followed two years later, and he was made a Knight of the Bath in 1725. But Lord Clinton was more than a courtier, and was active in political circles. From being originally a supporter of Robert Walpole, he changed allegiance, and opposed Walpole's Excise Bill in 1733. Walpole was forced to drop the Bill but got his revenge by dismissing from their posts in one day two dukes, four earls and two barons, including Clinton who found himself relieved of his post as Gentleman of the Bedchamber, and later replaced as Lord Lieutenant. However, upon Walpole's resignation in 1742, Lord Clinton's star was once again in the ascendancy, and in 1746 he was made first Baron Fortescue of Castle Hill, and the first Earl Clinton. As he died unmarried he was also the last.

*Hugh, 1st Earl Clinton, 1st Baron Fortescue.* Courtesy Lady Arran

In between his political activities, Hugh, Lord Clinton, found time to turn his attentions to the family home. It was his intention to consolidate his Devon estates, and to build them up he sold land in Somerset and Wiltshire to the value of £22,000, and £8000 in other parts of Devon, including Wood Barton near Kentisbeare, and instead bought up land around the Filleigh estate. The old medieval house which had been restyled a hundred years earlier, was largely or completely demolished, and the present Castle Hill built in its place and the landscaping of the grounds begun.

Lord Clinton was also involved in local politics, giving, it is said, the large sum of 500 guineas to Barnstaple Borough, ostensibly with no strings attached, but presumably hoping for some influence at election time. Elections were very expensive and when a member of the Fortescue family stood for the Opposition in 1747, the cost to Lord Clinton was reckoned to be some £3273, with an additional £1800 from the Prince of Wales.

Despite all this, their man did not get in, the seat going instead to Sir Bourchier Wrey by six votes, so presumably he had spent a similar sum of money. As there were only 322 voters, someone must have done very well out of it!

Lord Clinton died in 1751, aged only fifty-six. Although unmarried, he had built a house on the estate for his mistress and had at least one illegitimate child, a daughter who later married a cousin. With him died the Clinton earldom, and the Clinton barony went into abeyance, but the Fortescue lands, estates and title, by special remainder, passed to his half-brother Matthew, then aged thirty-two.

Matthew continued his brother's work on the house and particularly the grounds, and when he died thirty-two years later, passed on to his son, Hugh, an enviable inheritance. For fifty-six years Hugh, the third baron, held sway over Filleigh and much of the South Molton area. George III was on the throne when he succeeded, and when he died in 1841, Queen Victoria was four years into her long reign. As Lord Lieutenant, a post he held for fifty-one years from 1788, he was responsible for the visit of George III to Plymouth in 1789, and it was on this occasion that his sovereign created him Earl Fortescue. The family still have the robes made for the ceremony at a cost of £8 10s, and now faded to a respectable crimson, in contrast to the bright scarlet of peers of later creations!

As Lord Lieutenant, Lord Fortescue was responsible also for raising from the local farming population a local militia to counter the threat of Napoleonic invasions. In Devon as a whole, from a population of 340,000, 15,000 volunteers were raised, including 12,000 infantrymen and 1000 cavalry. Detailed organisation was put in place for the evacuation of women and children, and the removal of stock out of Boney's way, but so as not to block the roads for the movement of troops towards the coast, they were to take to the fields, removing gates and hedges as necessary. Presumably the invasion threat was expected in the summer months. In the days before a regular police force it also fell to the Lord Lieutenant to maintain law and order, and this could mean calling upon the local yeomanry in times of trouble, not uncommon during this period of unrest and agricultural depression.

Following the family tradition the eldest son was also called Hugh, and as Viscount Ebrington, entered Parliament in 1804, representing Barnstaple, and then the county. In 1820 he was sponsored by the Reform Party for the Tavistock seat which he held, and made an historic speech in support of Reform following the Act's rejection by the House of Lords. In the General Election that followed the Act's eventual passage, he stood unopposed for the newly created seat of North Devon, which he held until called to the House of Lords in 1839 when he was sent to Ireland as Viceroy. Since 1832 he had been assisting his ageing father in his post in the county. The first earl died in 1841.

By now the estate extended to some 30,000 acres, which produced a considerable income. The expenses the second earl had to find as head of the family were considerable, and included £2200 for his mother, who lived to be ninety-two; £1700 for his two brothers, and the costs and allowances of his own family. Nevertheless, he decided to buy from Sir Frederick Knight the reversion of the former Royal Forest of Exmoor, at what he considered to be an extortionate price and from that time, the family had a home at Simonsbath and great sporting interests over 20,000 acres of Exmoor. In 1856 he received 'a most kind offer of the Garter' from Lord Palmerston. It was an offer which he had previously refused, and when he died in 1861 a county subscription for a memorial raised over £1500, half of which was donated to the North Devon Infirmary, and as a result a statue of the second earl stands in Exeter Castle Yard.

Life must have seemed so certain for the landed gentry; Hugh the second had in due course succeeded his father, and his own son, Hugh the third, duly inherited and followed the familiar path of JP, DL and MP from 1841 until 1859 when he was appointed Lord of the Treasury. In 1847 he married his long-suffering wife, Georgiana Dawson-Damer who presented him with seven sons and as many daughters. She died in 1866, aged forty, giving birth to her seventh son. This enormous family produced some worthy sons. Seymour, the fifth son, was a naval captain and served three monarchs as equerry and was knighted for his services. He saw active service in Egypt and South Africa (as ADC) and his many decorations included the Legion of Honour. Lionel, the third son, was killed in the Boer War, and the youngest son, William, was lost aboard HMS *Wasp* in the China Seas in 1887. The fourth son, Arthur, was a captain in the Coldstream Guards, and his eldest son Grenville was killed in 1915. John, the second son, was very different. He was scholarly and seems to have been appointed to lectureships in Edinburgh, Oxford, Cambridge and London universities. He is best remembered as the Historian of the British Army and Librarian at Windsor Castle, for which he was knighted, but he was also a prolific author, writing mainly about the North Devon he knew and loved, its wildlife and its age-old customs and several delightful children's books.

By now the life of the Fortescue earls seems to have followed almost a set pattern. The eldest son, Hugh the fourth, before succeeding in 1905, entered Parliament. He became Lord Lieutenant in 1904 (until 1928) and served as ADC to both Edward VII and George V, and his wife, the Hon. Emily Ormsby-Gore was an Extra Lady of the Bedchamber to Queen Mary.

Hugh the fifth succeeded in 1932 and took up the by now traditional post of Lord Lieutenant in 1936, which he held all through the years of the Second World War right up until his death. He had seen active service in the First World War, and was twice wounded, and like so many of his family, much decorated. He took a more passive role in the next conflict as Col of the General Staff, and also as Lord in Waiting. Lady Fortescue worked tirelessly throughout, running the Women's Land Army, the Red Cross, the WVS etc., and after the war became president of the WCA, for which she was awarded the CBE.

*Three generations – the 4th earl, his son Viscount Ebrington, the future 5th earl, and his grandson, Peter, killed in action at El Alamein.*

Courtesy Lady Arran

*Viscount Ebrington.*

*Lady Margaret Fortescue.*

Tragedy came with the death of their only son, Peter, Viscount Ebrington, who was killed at El Alamein in 1942, a shock from which neither of them ever quite recovered. After the war the fifth earl was appointed Captain of the Gentleman at Arms, which is the equivalent of the Chief Whip in the House of Lords, and in 1951 was made a Knight of the Garter, the second of the family to be so honoured. He decided to hand over Ebrington to his younger brother Denzil, who succeeded him as sixth earl and whose son would ultimately become the seventh earl. At the same time he made his elder daughter, Lady Margaret, heir to Castle Hill and the Filleigh estates, giving Elizabeth, the younger daughter, the Weare Giffard house and lands. Lady Margaret remembers a very different world, although by the time she moved into Castle Hill with her parents, it was wartime, so the casual life of country house parties and endless entertaining had already ceased. Instead there was a boys' prep school from Sussex in residence. Before the war there had always been plenty of staff, although Lady Margaret remembers her mother thought she was dreadfully deprived when the numbers sunk to three in each department – only nine resident staff! The estate had its own building department, and she recalls that they mixed their own paints so that the distinctive golden hue of Castle Hill, of which one fifth was painted annually, could be somewhat uneven in appearance...

The dreadful Lynmouth flood disaster of 1954 had a great impact, and Lady Margaret remembers her father setting off to try to reach the devastated area. As Lord Lieutenant he was responsible, with the Lord Lieutenant for Somerset, for organising the relief aid, and all kinds of parcels kept arriving at Castle Hill, from kippers to cardigans. The appeal raised a massive sum which was invested, and continues to this day. As a fund-raising event, the two Lords Lieutenant organised a charity cricket match at Castle Hill with a few famous cricketing names as a draw. Everyone was completely taken by surprise when 3000 people turned up to watch.

In 1958 Lady Margaret was faced with an appalling dilemma. Her parents died within four days of each other, her mother having died first leaving everything to her husband. The death duties were monumental, and the only way to raise the sum required was to sell. All the Challacombe estate, a large part of Exmoor and a large part of West Buckland went, leaving the land near South Molton as the remaining estate today.

The church contains some interesting memorials, one to the two women who lost their lives in the fire that devastated Castle Hill in 1934. The close links between the Fortescues and their staff is demonstrated by the memorial to John Newton, whose father, mother, only brother and widow were each in service at Castle Hill...

> ...in the service of the first earl in 1860 and who died serving the third earl in 1899 and who wishes to record his grateful remembrance of fifty-nine years of faithful service and devoted attachment to himself and five generations of his family.

Castle Hill, whose, long elegant facade is such a familiar sight to all travellers on the former main road between South Molton and Barnstaple, suffered a disastrous fire in 1934. During the 1840s an attic storey had been added to house additional staff and nursery, and it is fortunate the family were away from home, otherwise these inaccessible rooms would have been occupied by staff and children. The fifth earl had only recently installed various improvements including a central heating boiler situated beneath the library floor. In the early hours of 9 March fire was discovered. It raged for two days and took the combined efforts of four fire brigades to bring it under control. The housekeeper and one of the maids lost their lives. The staff made heroic attempts at rescue and managed to save a great number of the contents of the ground floor, including the library carpet, but all the books were destroyed and most of the beautiful interiors were gone for ever, commemorated in a *Country Life* article due to appear later that month. It shows exquisite eighteenth-century interiors, with a double height saloon, highly decorative plaster mouldings and ceiling, decorative door cases and pediments and beautiful carpets.

Castle Hill was rebuilt with its original roof line, but the interiors could never be replicated. Another thing that the Fortescues are short on is ancestral portraits. By an unbelievable stroke of bad luck 49 paintings, which had been sent away to be restored after the fire, were returned but the van bringing them back arrived too late to be unloaded and so was parked in a

*Fire at Castle Hill in 1934.*

garage. During the night both lorry and garage went up in smoke, and 49 priceless paintings with them.

Lady Margaret married Bernard van Cutsem in 1948, divorced in 1968 and resumed her family name. Much of her life has been spent at Filleigh continuing her family's long tradition of dedication to the locality and the estate and those who live and work there. She was the first ever woman member of the CLA Devon branch and the first woman to be President of the Devon County Show, which she says was completely exhausting. In 1990 she handed over to her elder daughter Eleanor, who with her husband the ninth Earl of Arran, now lives at Castle Hill. Lady Arran supports many local charities and schools, and in 1994 was High Sheriff. She is President of the North Devon Hospice Trust and the Devon Gardens Trust. She intends to follow on from her mother, continuing her great interest and care of the estate. Lord Arran's interests have included publishing, gardening and sports, and following many of his forebears who have been involved in politics, his main career has been in the House of Lords with many Ministerial appointments. He remains one of the hereditary peers in the House of Lords. They have two daughters who have taken the name of Fortescue-Gore.

*Lord and Lady Arran.*

# FULFORD *of Great Fulford*

If any of the Fulford ancestors came back today, they would have no difficulty in recognising their family home of Great Fulford. The Fulfords of the twenty-first century live in their great quadrangular mansion pretty much as their forebears did, the only sops to modernity being electric light, a pleasant family kitchen, the odd computer and central heating, which is turned on only in dire necessity. Large houses are for youngsters says the current owner, Francis Fulford; they do not feel the cold and run around more. The Fulfords have been in possession of this unfrequented corner of Devon in unbroken male line for eight-hundred years and none of them had central heating.

Francis Fulford is a man of decided, and sometimes unusual opinions. He holds very much to the view that the best way of keeping one's inheritance intact is to do as little as possible, and certainly nothing entrepreneurial. Not for him the public walking through his rooms or bridal parties on the lawns, and certainly not American guests staying overnight to sample an ancestral home of the feudal era. (There would not be enough bathrooms anyway.) He is not against swelling the coffers with some commercial activities; Great Fulford has featured in several television productions, and the elegant wallpaper in the dining room came courtesy of the manufacturer who used the room for promotional purposes. Otherwise life continues at Great Fulford in a jolly, unsophisticated way. It is not, he stresses, that he minds any of these activities, it is just that he feels before embarking on turning one's home into an attraction, it pays to be sure that a decent return on the investment will accrue, and that the investment in the first place was of benefit to the house.

*One of the Saracens that have guarded the arms of Fulford since 1453.*

The first Fulford of note was William de Fulford who lived at the time of Richard I, and although often credited with accompanying him on his Crusade to the Holy Land, there is no evidence that he did so. Three-hundred years later came Sir Baldwin:

> *A great soldier and traveller of undaunted resolution that for the honour and liberty of a royal lady in a castle besieged by infidels, he fought a combat with a Saracen for bulk and bigness an unequal match (as the representation of him cut in the wainscot at Fulford House does plainly show) yet he vanquished and rescued the lady.*

This supposedly happened in 1453 and two Saracens have supported the arms of Fulford ever since.

Sir Baldwin had already served as Sheriff of Devon in 1438 in the time of Henry VI, as a Knight of the Sepulchre, and was appointed Under-Admiral to John Holland, Duke of Exeter and Admiral of England. On his return to England, he became embroiled in the Wars of the Roses and was a prominent Lancastrian. Together with his son Sir Thomas (who was knighted at the Battle of Wakefield), he fought at Towton and escaped, but after being betrayed by a Dartmouth gentleman named Staplehill, was tried for treason at Bristol and hung, drawn and quartered in 1461. All his estates were forfeited and Fulford house became for a time a Staplehill property.

Sir Thomas decided to redress the matter and in 1465 stormed Fulford House.

> One Sir Thomas Fulford with some two-hundred persons arrayed in ammer of war came... and did break into the house and did sore beat and grievously wound the servants... and so menaced the wife of your beseecher that she was in fear of her life.

Sir Thomas was prominent throughout the Yorkist years, despite his father's execution, and was given military and naval commands by both Edward IV and Richard III. He had a tendency to revert to the Lancastrian cause but seems to have been forgiven, until he backed the Duke of Buckingham in his rebellion against Richard III. When it failed he fled to Brittany. On the accession of Henry VII he was again in favour and his son Humphrey became a Squire of the King's Body and later a Knight of Bath, but died without issue.

*The beautiful tomb of Sir Thomas Fulford and his lady, Ursula in Dunsford church. He died in 1610, and she in 1639, the daughter of Richard Bampfield of Poltimore. They are surrounded by their numerous progeny.*

His brother opted for a safer life and entered the Church, becoming a canon of Exeter. Of his sisters, one married Wise of Sydenham and their daughter Alicia married John Russell and thus was the mother of the first Earl of Bedford. Another sister married William Cary of Cockington, who was killed at the Battle of Tewkesbury in 1471, but their grandson Lord Hunsdon, became Lord Chamberlain to Edward VI.

Sir Humphrey was succeeded by his brother William who married Joan Bonville so that the blood of this once great family runs in the veins of the Fulfords. By the time of Henry VIII they were sufficiently back in favour for Sir John, whose wife was Lady Dorothy Bourchier, daughter of the first Earl of Bath, to be appointed Sheriff in 1562. Sir John was responsible for the rebuilding of Fulford House and most of what is now visible is a result of his work, though it is certain that under the sixteenth-century skin much of the earlier house survives.

During the Civil War the Fulfords supported the Royalist cause. The head of the family, Colonel Sir Francis Fulford, spent much of the war in Dorset where the family had another estate but his sons fought in Devon. The house was initially stormed and sacked by Parliamentarians in 1642 and his younger son Francis captured and imprisoned in Exeter. When Exeter fell to the Royalists, though, he was freed. Colonel Thomas Fulford, his elder brother was killed in the siege.

Fulford House was later garrisoned for the king. After holding out for ten days, Colonel Okey won the day for the Parliamentarians and the Fulfords moved out for the second time in their history, whilst the house was garrisoned for the Roundheads. When they did regain possession Colonel Francis Fulford began a major refurbishment of the interior, but died young without issue and the estates passed to a cousin.

Francis (b.1704), married Anne Chichester of Youlston and it was the eighth of their eleven children who inherited. Squire John, who was responsible for the lovely lake in front of the house, spent money like water to such an extent that he was forced to move to France to live at less expense. All this before he was thirty! When he died in 1789, the property again went to a nephew.

*Col Thomas Fulford killed at the Siege of Exeter.*

*Great Fulford House.*

Baldwin (or Benjamin) was a great agricultural improver as well as being a soldier, who became a Lieutenant Colonel of the Devon Militia during the Napoleonic Wars. He spent largely on the house, gothicising the facade and some of the rooms around 1805. This was the generation that sent its sons around the world; one brother, John, became Admiral Fulford, and his son died of wounds in Peshaw in India in 1882. A younger brother, William, was a major in the Royal Artillery, and his son served throughout the entire Indian Mutiny, dying in Calcutta in 1858. But the second brother Francis entered the Church and emigrated to Canada, where in 1850 he was consecrated Bishop of Montreal, and ten years later, Metropolitan Bishop of Canada. He was also an eminent naturalist and was President of the Natural History Society of Montreal for many years. He died in 1868 and it was his son, another Francis, who would eventually come home to rescue Fulford's fortunes in 1890. He had settled in Montreal where he was a JP and a captain in the Montreal Cavalry and married to a Montreal girl. Sadly, Baldwin's son, 'Bad Baldwin' as he is known in the family, took after his Great-Uncle John rather than his prudent father, and by 1863 had accumulated such a mountain of debt to the tune of £60,000, that he ended up in the debtors' prison in Exeter. On his release he fled to France and his family undertook to pay his debts on the condition that he left his estates to his nephew Francis, son of the Bishop of Montreal.

For the next twenty-five years Great Fulford was let until Francis decided that the finances were sufficiently stable for him to be able to afford to move back, which he did in 1890.

Francis Algernon followed a sober and hard-working lifestyle. He was a civil servant and after a spell as an inspector with the Board of Trade, became Private Secretary to the President of the Board of Agriculture. He served as a JP and when he died in 1926 the Fulford estates were looking in much better shape. His son, Anthony (b.1898), served as a soldier throughout the First World War and continued as Assistant Military Secretary in Egypt, served also in Palestine, and through the Second World War, before retiring as a member of the Honourable Corps of Gentlemen-at-Arms. He married late in life, to the widow of one of his brother officers, and he was sixty-two when his son was born. Antony Fulford died in 1969 when his son was seventeen. It was his mother who kept things together, making sacrifices in order that the estate should survive, taking a clear long-term view, and being good at choosing her professional helpers.

Francis Fulford, is philosophical about his ancestors, and says an estate can survive one bad 'un every hundred years, but if you are unlucky enough to have two, then, 'You end up living in a farmhouse with 500 acres.' His family, he considers, have largely been solid performers, rarely stars, who have held together the estates despite the appalling agricultural depression that started in 1875 and lasted for more or less a hundred years, yet still the Fulfords have 3000 acres. There are 12 tenant farmers, and 20 cottages or houses, which these days tend to be let out to people not connected with the estate, or the land 'The farmhouse used to be thrown in with the land, but nowadays if the farms have amalgamated, it makes much more sense to let it separately.' The estate is beautifully timbered and shooting is obviously important, although not in a large commercial way. All in all, he considers that the estate is profitable though not so profitable as he would wish. This man, who so obviously know his own lands inside out, talks figures that highlight the costs involved: £5000 per annum for electricity; a similar sum for general maintenance; council tax and water rates; and a prudent owner has a sinking fund against the time a new roof is required. If an estate brings in £200,000 per annum, the order for the new Jaguar must come after the wages bill, insurance, accountants and bank fees, school fees and household expenses, which bring it down to around £40,000 before tax. This leaves the owner with between £20 and £40,000 per year. And then, there is the roof.

*The Fulford coat of arms supported by two Saracens still tops an ancient entrance.*

Frances Fulford (the twenty-seventh of that name to own the estate) was born in 1952, and led an interesting and varied life before settling down at Great Fulford. A spell in the Coldstream Guards was followed by a few years in Australia on a cattle ranch. He found City life difficult but stayed with it, ending up running a Lloyd's Reinsurance brokerage. He had always maintained that he would not come back to Great Fulford to live until he was married. His wife is Kishanda, named after a beautiful valley in Tanganyika where her father was District Commissioner. The couple have four children and Francis aims to be in a position to hand over the estate to his son in good order and considers that the omens are looking better than they have done for a very long time. Margaret Thatcher, he considers, did more to save the country estate than anyone else for a long time, and owning a country estate is now becoming fashionable, so that values are increasing, after long, long years in the doldrums when they were considered far more of an albatross than an asset.

All in all, he concludes:

*those of us who own great estates and are used to playing the long game will reflect on our good fortune to have had fathers and grandfathers and great-grandfathers who somehow managed to weather the appallingly turbulent years between 1875 and 1979 so that the estate continues today in much better shape.*

*Francis Fulford, the present owner, and his son, Francis Arthur.*

# FURSDON *of Fursdon*

atriona Fursdon thought her life would follow a settled pattern after her marriage to David Fursdon in 1987. He was a civil servant with the Ministry of Defence and they moved into a house in Highgate in London. Six months later she found herself as chatelaine of Fursdon, a house she had visited only once before. David Fursdon took over from his Uncle John, who without children of his own to succeed, had decided to pass the house and estate over to his nephew and new young wife.

'It was all so unexpected,' Catriona recalls. 'The house seemed so big, and there hadn't been any children at Fursdon for fifty years, and it had been lived in by older people who used less of the house.' One fact soon became crystal clear. Far from the estate keeping them, they would have to keep the estate. The Civil Service career went, and David Fursdon took up a teaching post at nearby Blundell's school in Tiverton. Catriona set about the task of renovating the house.

*David and Catriona Fursdon and their children.*

Courtesy David Fursdon

*Fursdon House.*
Courtesy David Fursdon

When their first son Oliver was born in 1980, he was the first Fursdon to be born in the house for two-hundred years. Next came Tom in 1982, then Charlie in 1987. All three have been educated at Blundell's and Oliver is now reading History at Edinburgh University while Tom is at Cambridge reading Land Economics.

The family can first be found at Fursdon in records dating to the days of Henry III. From Walter de Fursdon, known to have been living at Fursdon in 1259, the estate has passed in unbroken male line down to the present day. The steep, hilly country between Tiverton and Crediton seems always remote, and the quiet lane leading to the estate is a typical narrow Devon lane between high banks, contouring along a valley side and passing the gateway almost by accident. There is nothing grand, no lodge or ornate gate piers, just an unassuming white gate opening on to a short drive. Neither is the house grand. It has an elegant, pleasing colonnaded front, added in the nineteenth century, behind which is a house that has grown over the centuries. The earliest evidence dates from the late sixteenth century with an H-shaped house consisting of a great hall and two flanking wings.

In the same quiet fashion, tending their Devon acres and minding their own business, the Fursdons have survived, usually more interested in local and family matters than affairs of state; great positions and great glories also carry great risks, as other families have found to their cost.

There have been one or two close shaves, as when George (there have been nine George Fursdons) died in 1722 leaving an only son barely one year old, to inherit. There have been several strong-minded wives to bring both their fortunes and their willpower to the family, and outstanding was Grace Fursdon. Widowed in 1643 when her husband was killed fighting for Charles I near Lyme Regis, she brought up her family, including the heir, Nicholas, then aged eight, but held the reins of Fursdon until her death in 1691.

*Grace Fursdon.*

Courtesy David Fursdon

*George Fursdon 1690–1740.*

Courtesy David Fursdon

*George Fursdon 1802–1872.*

Courtesy David Fursdon

She was a redoubtable figure, one of those commanding, competent women who strike terror into most male breasts. She completely took over and held together the family, managing the estates and finances with considerable skill. When she died, she left an estate worth £20,000. As a reward for the family's loyalty to the Crown – she is known to have lent Charles I £20 – there are preserved at Fursdon several items of pewter given by Charles II. It is said that Grace's ghost appears on the balcony on the anniversary of the execution of Charles I, and that her spirit still watches over the Fursdons.

By the time Grace's grandson, George, inherited in 1714, the estates were considerable and it was a time of agricultural wealth and rising incomes. George set about bringing the house up to date in line with the fashion of the day. A new wing was built on to the eastern end, replacing some of the old kitchens, and a new entrance built in the centre of the south front. His son, also George, became High Sheriff and Deputy Lieutenant, and his sword, and a copy of his oath, and pipe roll are all preserved at Fursdon. George's first wife was Elizabeth Cheyney, a lady of considerable fortune who married George in 1753. She died young, however, and George married again, to Grace Sydenham, from Combe Sydenham in Somerset, and lived just long enough to beget his only son, another George, born in 1771.

When he came of age, George Sydenham Fursdon also made alterations to the house, adding a bedroom floor to the great hall, moving the front door to the rear and adding a smaller entrance door to one side of the front door and creating a new staircase hall. He later added the library wing, and in 1818 the new ionic colonnade was added to the front of the house.

George died in 1836, and was succeeded by his son George (b.1802) who would appear to have been the black sheep of the family. Not only did he gamble away most of his own fortune, but also that of his wife, the daughter of a wealthy sugar plantation owner. On the plus side, he built the stables, planted many of the fine trees, including the cedars, and was keenly interested in the excavation of the ancient earthwork at Cadbury Castle, above the house. However, so bad did things become, that George was forced to leave Fursdon, and let his brother Edward, the vicar of Dawlish, take over the running of the estate. It was not until Edward's death in 1869 that George's son, Charles, regained possession of the house and estate. Between them the two brothers had a total of 17 children.

This was a period of financial difficulty for the family. They had relied in part on the wealth brought in by the copper mine at South Zeal, which in 1862 raised 175 tons of ore, valued at £1036 and more than double the following year. In 1873 the total was £4404, but it was discovered that the manager had been quietly embezzling much of the money. Decline set in and in 1891 the mine was abandoned. Charles who, with his wife Eliza, had to steer the family through this period, was content to live quietly at Fursdon where he became a keen and knowledgeable farmer. He was an acknowledged authority on livestock and installed an early version of the

*George Henry Fursdon (1859–1942) and his wife, Charlotte (d.1935).*
Courtesy David Fursdon

hydraulic ram to raise water to the fields. He died in 1912, just before the First World War and it fell to his son, George Henry, to struggle to keep things going, without any help as all the workers had left to fight, and his own son, George Ellaworth, was away fighting. Although he survived and returned home, he died in 1936, six years before his father, leaving a widow, Aline, and three children. With the outbreak of the Second World War, Aline and her family moved into Fursdon with her father-in-law, by then in his eighties, and with the help of a cook, one maid and a garden boy, she ran the house. (George) John, her eldest son, volunteered the day war broke out. He was invalided home in 1942, just months before his grandfather died. At that time, Fursdon was completely unmodernised, without electricity or proper plumbing, and what the evacuees who moved down must have thought of it is not recorded. The Army also used the house at one stage, but it survived both intrusions; what nearly finished the Fursdon's long tenure were the death duties incurred in 1942. John struggled on, and began his own forestry business, which grew out of a desire to replace the trees felled during the war, and has had the great satisfaction of living long enough to see some of his plantings reach maturity. For some time Fursdon was let whilst John was running a bird observatory in Wales, but he realised that only its owners would properly care for the old house and that he would have to move back. He did not marry until 1968, and with his wife, Christine, began the conversion of the back part of the house to self-catering flats. It was his aim to share Fursdon, and attract people who were also keen nauralists. With Christine's deteriorating health, and the knowledge that it would be his brother's son, David, who would ultimately inherit, John decided to pass the estate over in 1981.

*Charles Fursdon 1829–1912.*
Courtesy David Fursdon

Catriona has become fascinated with the history of her home and is keen to have it fully researched and recorded, aware that there is so much to find out and so little has been disturbed. Over their twenty years of tenure, she and her husband have worked remarkable changes. In common with other owners, they have found it necessary to open Fursdon to the public on 30 days every year as this is a principal condition of the exemption of some of the inheritance tax, which would otherwise have been crippling.

'We decided if we were going to do it, we would do it properly,' Catriona stated. The house is now open more than the minimum requirement and Catriona and her team have put a great deal of work into it, for which she obviously has considerable flair. Redundant kitchen quarters and the former billiard room have been converted into a family museum with a display of old family costumes, baby clothes and military costumes and a variety of items dating from the Civil War.

The house has been systematically restored and rejuvenated. The hall and staircase hall now have a specially woven carpet, designed by Catriona herself, based on the panelling in the dining room, originally the great parlour. She has been her own interior designer throughout and whilst David Fursdon has been quietly keeping the family fortunes afloat, working now as a partner in the auctioneer firm of Stags, his wife has been the guiding hand behind the creation of a modern family home and a tourist attraction at the same time. 'We open in the summer and do cream teas for parties, and although I would hate to be open all the year, I do miss the visitors once we have shut. It is fun showing them round and sharing Fursdon with them.'

All that is left of the estate is 750 acres surrounding the house which includes the Home Farm which is farmed in hand. At one time they owned extensive lands around the Crediton and Exe Valley areas, including Raddon Court at Thorverton where another branch of the family lived in the seventeenth century.

◇◇ ◆ ◇◇

# GILBERT *of Compton Castle*

## *Quid non* – Why Not?

The Gilberts are another of Devon's remarkable seafaring families whose sons went forth from their sleepy little fishing villages to discover new countries and new seas, and to fight great battles, defending the honour of their queen and country. The most famous member of the family was Sir Humphrey Gilbert, born at Greenway in 1539, a house on the Dart estuary within sound of the sea. His mother was Katherine Champernowne, whose second marriage produced another renowned son, Sir Walter Raleigh. Is there any other county that has produced in one generation such a roll-call of famous sons as sprung from Devon in the days of Elizabeth I?

Compton Castle came into the Gilbert family when Joan de Compton married Geoffrey, son of Thomas Gilbert of Totnes. Geoffrey represented Totnes in Parliament in 1326 and seems to have been some form of tax collector for the king, required to raise money from the abbots and priors (always a good source of revenue) to help defray the expenses of the war against the Scots. William, his grandson, was a ship owner, licensed to carry pilgrims to Santiago and back. The Gilberts were rising in importance, for his son, Otho Gilbert, was appointed Sheriff in 1475, and it was

*Compton Castle, around 1975, by Nicholas Horne.*

Courtesy G. Gilbert

in his time that the castle was enlarged and rebuilt to appear substantially as it stands today. Along with many other familiar Devon names such as Bourchier, Champernowne, Courtenay and Fulford, he was active in the wars against France and was commissioned to 'arrest ships as necessary' for the safe conduct of the Army.

His grandson, also Otho, lived at Greenway, and when he succeeded his uncle, both estates were combined. Like many of his contemporaries, Otho was a ship owner involved in maritime affairs and his three sons, John, Humphrey and Adrian, led full and active lives, all of them bound up with the sea, and all of them playing a prominent part on the maritime stage.

Sir John, who lived at the then principal residence of Greenway, was much involved in Humphrey's activities. He seems not to have been at sea so much himself but was regularly involved in county administration and Admiralty work, and was Vice Admiral for Devon, busy with the defence against the Armada invasion threat. He was also influential at court and something of a favourite with Queen Elizabeth so that he was in the right place at the right time to put in a word for brother Humphrey. There is a fine effigy of him and his wife in Exeter Cathedral, a rare honour.

*Sir Humphrey Gilbert.*
Devon & Exeter Institution

Humphrey Gilbert, the middle son, was educated at Eton and Oxford, and he was far more than a bluff sailor. To persuade those in influence to back him on a voyage of discovery seeking a North-West route to open up the wealth of the eastern hemisphere, in 1566 he prepared a 'Discourse for the Discovery of a New Passage to Cataia' (China) – a kind of early business plan. This was hopefully presented to the queen, but nothing came of it, so Humphrey returned to Ireland where he was serving and where he was knighted by the Lord Deputy, Sir Henry Sidney. He must have been an enlightened man, for on his return from the expeditions to the Low Countries, he prepared and again presented to the queen a proposal for a form of university especially for training the sons of the nobility and those who were wards of the Crown for the Navy and the Army, to be called Queen Elizabeth's Academy. Had his proposal been adopted, Britain would have had military and naval colleges centuries before any other country. Sir Humphrey considered it would prepare boys' minds to deal with emergencies, they would study charts and engineering, and also history which Sir Humphrey considered to be the key to 'all noble exploits that ever were or are to be done'. Alas, the scheme failed because the queen would not pay the instructors.

His next treatise was on 'How to annoy the King of Spain', no doubt much more to the queen's liking. A year later, in 1578 she granted Sir Humphrey Letters Patent to found an English colony. Together with Thomas Carew and Walter Raleigh, he amassed a fleet of seven vessels for exploration and possible colonisation, funded by, among others, Sir Francis Walsingham, but difficulties beset them from the start and the expedition had eventually to be abandoned amidst accusations and counter-accusations of piracy. Such expeditions relied to a large extent on the 'prizes' won at sea so there was fierce competition, but without such prizes, there was no financial reward for the backers or for the sailors themselves. This was the first such to be blessed by Queen Elizabeth, who had granted Sir Humphrey licence to search out 'remote heathen and barbarous lands not actually possessed of any Christian peoples – to have, hold, occupy and enjoy with all commodities, jurisdiction and royalties...' Rich prizes were indeed at stake.

However, when things went wrong, as they had done, it could mean financial hardship. Such was Sir Humphrey's case and he found himself so hard up that 'he even had to sell the clothes from off his wife's back'. At the time they were living in Bishopsgate, where their first son was born.

It took Sir Humphrey five years to get together another expedition. The Gilbert brothers appear to have been high in their queen's esteem for via Sir Walter Raleigh, she gave Sir Humphrey a jewel of a golden anchor with a pearl and her personal good wishes for his safety. Five vessels, including the *Golden Hind*, set sail from Plymouth in June 1583, arriving on the far shore of the Atlantic in August. Here Sir Humphrey landed at St John's, in the New Found Land, and claimed it for Queen Elizabeth, setting up a post with the Arms of England engraved in lead, thus effectively founding the first British colony.

With a three-month sea voyage between him and home, no time was to be lost, so Sir Humphrey turned south down the coast, no doubt looking for future sites for colonies. One of his ships, the *Delight*, was forced ashore in a gale, and sank with the loss of nearly 100 lives, and all Gilbert's papers and plans, a sad blow to the expedition. Despite worsening weather, Sir Humphrey turned for home, deciding to sail on the smallest vessel of his fleet, the *Squirrel*. She was quite unable to cope with the mountainous seas encountered near the Azores, and foundered with the loss of all aboard her, including Sir Humphrey who was heard to cry out, 'We are as near to heaven by sea or by land.' 'For the wings of man's life are plumed with the feathers of death,' he had told his sovereign several years earlier. He left behind a family of nine sons and one daughter, to whom the childless Sir John now became a father.

Adrian, the youngest brother, took on Humphrey's mantle, and in turn received Letters Patent from Elizabeth in 1584 to explore the passage to China. With many famous seafaring and West Country names he formed the 'Fellowship for Discovery of the North-West Passage'.

Humphrey's eldest son, John, accompanied his uncle, Sir Walter Raleigh, who had carried on where Humphrey left off, and continued the process of colonisation in the New World, sailing with him in 1595 to Guiana. The following year he was aboard with Sir Walter during the historic destruction of the Spanish fleet off Cadiz and fought so valiantly that he was knighted for his part. Only two years later he became Admiral of the Western Coast and had command of the royal vessel, the *Antelope*. His last post was as Governor of Fort Plymouth, and when he died in 1608 in London, his body was brought back to Compton and buried in Marldon church.

By now, King James had succeeded to Elizabeth's throne and in 1606 the young Raleigh Gilbert, Sir Humphrey's youngest son, was continuing the family traditions. He was one of eight granted the right to set up colonies in Virginia and a year later he set sail from Plymouth with two ships and 120 would-be settlers. The colony they founded, called Fort St George on the coast of Maine, did not succeed. One of the leaders and several of the settlers died during the first winter, so that when news came of the death of his uncle, Sir John Gilbert, which meant that Raleigh now inherited Compton, he and the settlers decided to return home, sailing in a vessel they had constructed themselves. This would appear to be the last attempt of the Gilberts at colonisation, but Raleigh continued his naval career, and he, too, took part in an attack on Cadiz in 1625, in command of His Majesty's ship *St George*. He died in 1634.

Not much is known of the next two generations, except that the Sandridge estate, also on the Dart estuary, came into the family when Joan Pomeroy married Humphrey Gilbert. Their son, John, born 1684, married Anne Courtenay from Powderham, and it was he who sold Greenway, preferring to live at Sandridge. They had a large family of eight daughters and four sons and for the next five generations the Gilbert seafaring mould was broken; the eldest son, Pomeroy was a military man, and the last to live at Compton, and his eldest son, Edmund, moved to Cornwall as vicar of Constantine, and later Prebendary of Exeter. His brother's wife inherited the Bodmin Priory property which became the principal home of the Gilberts and passed eventually to Edmund's son, the Revd John Pomeroy Gilbert who was a Fellow of Exeter College, Oxford, vicar of St Wenn in Cornwall and like his father, a Prebendary of Exeter. The second son of this enormous family of 12, Walter Raleigh Gilbert, followed a military career, going to India at the age of fifteen as a Bengal Infantry cadet, and was soon embroiled in the various campaigns. By the time of the Sikh War in 1845, he was in command of the Second Division and was highly praised by his commander in chief. General Gilbert was again in command when the second Sikh War broke out, and it was to him that 16,000 Sikhs and 41 guns surrendered at Rawalpindi, bringing the war to an end. For this he was portrayed on the reverse of the medal issued to the serving troops, showing the Sikhs laying down their weapons before him; the Duke of Wellington is the only other general thus honoured. General Gilbert became a member of the Council of India in 1850, and was made a baronet in 1851. The obelisk erected on Bodmin Moor to his memory still stands. He left a son, Francis, who died childless, and two daughters, one of whom married the General's ADC and emigrated to New Zealand. The other married Captain (later General) Richard Shubrick and it was their daughter, Rachel, who married the Revd Walter Gilbert of Bodmin Priory, thus reuniting the two branches.

*The ruined Compton Castle in 1895 when it was one of the sights of the Torquay district.*

Compton Castle by this time was little more than a ruin. It had been sold off in 1785 to the Templars but even before then the great hall had been demolished and the building was in decline. With the death of Edmund in 1816 the Gilbert family departed from the Dart estuary, and from Devon. By the end of the nineteenth century, visitors were paying to wander around the picturesque ruins of the once mighty family home.

This, then, is what the Revd Walter Raleigh Gilbert's son saw in 1904. Aged fifteen, Walter Gilbert a young naval cadet, came over from Dartmouth, the first Gilbert to feel the call of the sea for a long time, and to take a look at the home of his illustrious ancestors. Young Gilbert never forgot the vow he made that one day he would buy back Compton Castle and restore it. The first step came in 1931 when he was able to purchase the castle and surrounding orchard. The tale of the reconstruction is fascinating. Commander Gilbert and his wife proceeded cautiously and meticulously, taking great pains over a long period of years to ensure that everything was as historically accurate as was possible. With help from relatives both in England and America, whilst also raising a family of four boys and a girl, they restored the house and bought back 365 acres of the former farm lands. The decision to rebuild the great hall was controversial, but has been proved to be a masterpiece, bringing together several traditional skills, such as the wrought ironwork to the windows and the gates, forged in the local smithy.

*Commander Walter Raleigh Gilbert by Denis Fildes.*  Courtesy G Gilbert

In 1951 Commander Gilbert handed over Compton Castle to the National Trust with the proviso that it should continue to be home to the Gilberts. His eldest son, Humphrey, had been killed in 1942. Commander Gilbert was married twice, and Ann and Humphrey were the children of the first marriage. Humphrey was a Spitfire pilot during the war, who fought in the Battle of Britain and was awarded a DFC. It is, therefore, his second son Geoffrey, who now lives at Compton Castle with his wife Angela and three children, Arabella, Humphrey and Walter Raleigh.

*Compton Castle restored.*

◇◇◆◇◇

# HEATHCOAT AMORY
## *of Tiverton*

### *Amre non vi* – By love not force

*John Heathcoat.*

Courtesy Sir Ian Amory Bt

The Heathcoat Amorys are newcomers to the Devon scene, relatively speaking. Their estates were not granted to them by the Conqueror, they did not figure on the field of Agincourt, or Bosworth, and their title was not conferred on them by a generously-minded monarch on his accession to the English throne. Instead they have risen from the ranks, and gained their position by hard-work and philanthropy. In 1826, Samuel Amory married Anne, daughter and co-heiress of John Heathcoat, and it was their son, John who first used the combined name and became the first baronet.

The Heathcoats were originally a Derbyshire farming family. John, born 1783, was apprenticed into the hosiery trade, but decided at an early age that lace was more to his liking. His first step to success was to go into partnership with his brother-in-law in Nottingham, and to secure his first patent. By 1808 he had bought out his partner with a staggering loan from a Derbyshire solicitor, perhaps as large as £20,000, and had started up on his own, designing and patenting the lace bobbin machine known as the 'Old Loughborough', the town to which he had moved from Nottingham. The dawn of the industrial age was a troublesome time, and although John Heathcoat foresaw there might be some problems, he never envisaged the wholesale destruction of his 55 looms in the space of around half an hour on 18 June 1816. The wreckers called it a 'proper Waterloo job'. John Heathcoat was offered compensation of £10,000, but with the proviso that he rebuilt in Loughborough. Somehow this did not appeal. Perhaps he was concerned for the safety of his wife and three children, perhaps for the safety of his workers. Whatever the reason, the whole enterprise of lace-making was moved down south to one of the former woollen mills on the River Exe at Tiverton. He realised that here was spare capacity and a work-force ready and willing to work with him. John Heathcoat must have already been displaying the philanthropic streak that set the family far apart from other mill owners of the time, for many of his former workers followed him on foot from Loughborough to take up positions in the new enterprise.

The factory prospered and expanded, and by the time his son-in-law, John Amory took over, it employed over 1000 workers and was the largest lace factory in the world. John Amory was the son of Samuel, banker and lawyer to John Heathcoat, whose daughter Anne he married. By this time Heathcoat had bought up large areas of land around the town, especially in the area of his factory for expansion, and for the building programme he initiated almost immediately for his workers. What amounts to a small estate of neat terraced houses of pleasing, plain elevations was built facing the factory and also leading up to St Paul's Church, which was built by Caroline, John Heathcoat's daughter who married Ambrose Brewin, his partner from Loughborough. The school, built in a sort of Tudor revival style, dates from around 1841, the first factory school to be opened in the West Country and firmly non-denominational.

By this time the family had moved to Bolham House, on the outskirts of Tiverton. John Heathcoat entered Parliament in the wake of the Great Reform Bill of 1832, and later he represented Tiverton with Palmerston. His over-riding concern was the welfare of his workers and the people of Tiverton, a far from fashionable view at the time. He was rewarded with the affection and respect of the town, and when he finally retired from public life in 1859, around 1300 of 'his people' presented him with a silver inkstand and golden pen 'as a tribute of gratitude and respect for the interest that he has always felt in their welfare and for his liberality to them on all occasions'. His death in 1861 marked the end of a remarkable man, whose invention revolutionised factory life throughout the Midlands, as well as the West Country, and whose principles and ideals caused a quieter, but equally far-reaching revolution in the treatment of workers.

*W.C.L. Unwin JP, partner in John Heathcoat & Co.*

His grandson, John Heathcoat Amory, being the third generation to have wealth, took less of an active interest in the running of the lace factory, and passed this over to his wife's brother, W.C.L. Unwin, who worked unceasingly from 1872 until 1917. By now, the family has become established, and John Heathcoat Amory became a Deputy Lieutenant of the County, JP and served as Liberal MP for Tiverton from 1869 until 1885. He took to the life

*Knightshayes Court.*

*Sir John, 1st Bt, married the only daughter of William Unwin.*

of a country squire with ease, keeping three packs of hounds – staghounds, foxhounds and harriers. In about 1860, a year before his grandfather's death, he bought the neighbouring Knightshayes estate. Nothing survives of the original Georgian house, because by 1869 when the foundation stone was laid, the Heathcoat Amorys had decided on an ambitious new house, high Victorian designed by the most eminent Gothic architect of the day, William Burgess. It is his high, imposing and dominating house that now looks down over the parkland to Tiverton and the mill from which their wealth originated, although Sir John, as he had now become, and his wife backed away from the ambitious and ornate interiors that were part of the original plans, settling instead for slightly more modest (and cheaper) alternatives from John Crace. By the time Sir John died in 1914, life seemed very satisfactorily settled for the family. They had introduced the first-ever pension scheme, and a profit-share scheme for their workers, who now numbered well over 1000, and two of his three sons, Ian and Ludovic, had joined the firm.

*'A Hunting Family', Sir John Heathcoat and his three sons and son-in-law.*
Courtesy Sir Ian Amory Bt

The First Word War claimed the life of Ludovic, and Sir Ian died in 1931 as a result of a hunting accident, by which time two of his sons, John and Derick had joined him on the Board. John remained Chairman until 1966, but the structure of the textile industry was changing fast, and in 1970 the firm became part of the Coats Patons Group. This, however, was not the end of the Heathcoat story. In the late 1960s, Heathcoats developed a new process producing a form of industrial fabric that once coated with rubber becomes the basis for drive belts. The original factory had been rebuilt after a disastrous fire in the 1940s, and in 1984 a new era began when John Heathcoat & Co was bought back from Coats Patons by a management team.

Together with his brother Derick, who later became Viscount Amory, Sir John set up the Heathcoat Trust endowing it with shares in the company. This trust still operates strongly and further endowments and wise investment mean that annually it is able to give substantial help to those in need, especially pensioners, with education and a wider range of charitable good causes. The philanthropic streak runs deep in the Heathcoat Amorys, and the present baronet is much involved in the administration of this trust as well as many other charitable causes.

Sir John married Joyce Wethered, one of the foremost lady golfers of her time. She was not too enamoured of the colourful decorative schemes at Knightshayes and caused some of them to be 'painted out'. Her great love was the garden, and together with her husband she began the creation of the splendid gardens that are what first attracted the National Trust to the property. They delighted in dispersing the formality of the garden they inherited but the garden they created was specifically a 'garden in a wood', rather than a woodland garden, a distinction they were very particular about. It was in part inspired by another remarkable garden created by an equally remarkable Amory wife before the First World War at Chevithorne, a beautiful Elizabethan house nearby. Ludovic had married May Bannatyne, and they had three sons before he was killed in 1918. Tragedy struck this family again and again; Michael was killed in a plane crash in 1936, Patrick was killed in action in Libya in 1942, and Gerald killed in action in Normandy in 1944. May lived on at Chevithorne, her life revolving around her garden and her grandchildren, Michael and Amanda, whose mother had remarried to an Amory cousin. Michael and his family still live at Chevithorne, and he and his wife, Arabella, carry on the gardening tradition: Chevithorne holds one of the national oak collections and the rest of the garden is continually being expanded and improved. His half-brother, David Heathcoat Amory continues another tradition as a Member of Parliament.

Derick Heathcoat Amory succeeded his brother as fourth baronet in 1972 by which time he was better known as Viscount Amory of Tiverton. He had followed a political career, sitting as the Conservative MP for Tiverton from 1945–60, with posts at the Ministry of Pensions, the Board of Trade as Minister of State, the Ministry of Agriculture & Fisheries, and as Chancellor of the Exchequer from 1958–60. Then followed three years as the High Commissioner for Canada where he became the Governor of the Hudson Bay Company. He returned to become President of John Heathcoat & Co in 1973, which position he held until his death in 1981. Both brothers were made Freemen of Tiverton, and both Viscount Amory and his father served on the County Council. The title then passed to the third brother, William, who died the following year. All three brothers had distinguished war records, and Sir William managed one of the family flour mills after retiring from the Army. When this was taken over by Rank Hovis McDougall,

*Calverleigh Court.*

Sir William 'retired to do good works', another habit of the family. It was Sir John, the third baronet, and his wife Joyce, who made the decision to pass Knightshayes over to the National Trust. They were the last Heathcoat Amorys to live in the house, and when the Trust took over, a comfortable house was made in the former staff wing, where she lived until her death in 1997. Although Sir Ian, the sixth baronet, visited Knightshayes frequently during the lifetime of his uncle and aunt, the first time he ever went upstairs was when his sister was married from there in 1961. He remembers family gatherings downstairs, where, in spite of its size, it always seemed warm and cosy. But home for him and his father was Calverleigh, bought by Viscount Amory just before the war from the Chichesters. The house was let as a school during the war, and when his cousin Patrick, who was being groomed to stand for Parliament, was killed during the war, Derick stood instead, and thereafter found he had little time or use for Calverleigh, so he gave it to his brother William, Ian's father, a serving soldier with the 60th Rifles. When in 1950 the family moved in, Sir Ian remembers a scholastic air everywhere and lots of pale green and cream paint which it took some time to replace.

There have been many changes in Sir Ian's lifetime. When he was born the family still owned and ran the textile factory, and still owned Knightshayes. Both are now in other hands, but what is left is more than enough to keep Sir Ian busy. He studied business management in America before joining the firm, and spent some time in the London sales office. He then qualified as an accountant, a sensible skill, but at this time the firm was sold off, and

*Sir Ian and Lady Amory and their four sons.* Courtesy Sir Ian Amory Bt

Sir Ian came home to run the remainder of the family business. He also devoted much of his time to local causes, serving for twelve years on the County Council and as a JP for thirteen years until 1993. Sir Ian was sorry to leave the County Council in 1985, but recalls Uncle Derick saying that ten years was enough for anyone to give of their best. Sir Ian left before an election that brought a sharp swing to the Liberals. As this door shut, that of the National Trust opened. He had joined the regional board in 1982, becoming Chairman in 1986 until 1996 and still sits on the National Council and Properties Committee. He also became a member of the Council for the Protection of Rural England, becoming President in 1998. Here he is working hard to raise the profile of the charity, stressing that they are not fighting just for purely parochial issues but for matters that affect everyone.

Calverleigh is a pleasant, cream stuccoed Regency house tucked away in a quiet valley on the outskirts of Tiverton with only a small church for a neighbour. The estate includes a few farms, all let out, and a modest shoot. Surrounding the house is a lovely and developing garden, for Sir Ian married another gardening lady, Louise Pomeroy. She is a direct descendant of Ralph de la Pomerai, an ancient family who settled in Devon after the Conquest.

Louise Amory is a strong supporter of Save the Children and both are happy for Calverleigh to be used for charitable fund-raising events, although the house remains very much a family home for themselves and their four sons.

◇◇◆◇◇

# KELLY *of Kelly*

*The Kelly family scroll.*
Courtesy the Kelly family

In a quiet and unfrequented corner of Devon that is almost Cornwall, where the high ground falls steeply to the fast-flowing water of the Tamar, is the village of Kelly. Tall trees surround the church and hide the old manor house, which has been the home of the Kelly family since at least the days of the Conquest, and where, with quiet determination, they still live. As Professor Hoskins wrote in *Devon:*

> *These parishes where old families have ruled for centuries have a flavour all their own, even a characteristic smell of wet, decaying plantations.*

Never once has the male line failed, and their straightforward genealogy has been recorded on a beautifully gilded and decorated scroll some 20 feet in length. Mrs Margery Kelly, widow of Michael Kelly, now occupies part of Kelly House, and her son Warrin lives in the stableblock with his son Jonathon, so that the line continues as it always has done.

The house is as remarkable as the family. The oldest part is the almost untouched medieval house characterised by its deep entrance porch with a room over, along with huge fireplaces and tiny windowpanes. Added on

*The medieval Kelly.*
Courtesy Kelly family

to it is a late Georgian four-square house, but without the usual grand entrance. Instead there is a small door to one side, and the principal rooms face in the opposite direction to the original house.

Inside is a collection of handsome rooms and a fine staircase with a few ancestral portraits gazing down on a house that has undeniably seen better days. The rest of the family consider that Margery Kelly is absolutely mad to stay on, in a house where the rain pours through the ceilings if the central gutter is not kept clear of debris, and where modernisation means that at least they have electric light, but not much else. She accepts that the next generation may not want to continue here, but as the very fine stable block is undergoing renovation, and, as Mrs Kelly put it, no one wants to be the Kelly to chuck in the towel and finally leave all those centuries of history behind, she stays on.

The 'new house'.

The past century has been a difficult time for the family. Robert Maitland Kelly was killed in 1917, and Nicholas, the elder brother, also died, leaving Michael and Margery to inherit. Unplanned death duties took a savage toll; almost the entire contents of the house had to be sold, and most of the land which at one time stretched down to the Tamar, to Dunterton and Greystone, and all of Kelly village. Grandfather Kelly sold off most of it, and the cottages in the village went for a pittance at the time when the tenants were demanding amenities such as running water, bathrooms and new roofs. It seemed cheaper at the time to sell them off!

Arthur Kelly, who died in 1875, was the last of the old order of hunting squires. There was nothing grand about him. Wearing old homespun clothes, he kept his own pack of hounds, and Kelly was open-house to all his hunting cronies. Even then, he was considered old-fashioned, and the state of the house was not nearly so important to him as the state of his hunters.

The stables.

*Revd Maitland Kelly, 'squarson' at Kelly for many years.*

Courtesy Kelly family

*Admiral Kelly.*

Kelly College, Tavistock

It had been the custom for the younger brother to become the rector of neighbouring Kelly church, the first being Nicholas de Kelly in 1297, but Arthur fell out with his younger brother and offered the living to a stranger, an action he later regretted but could not undo, and thus the two brothers were estranged for a long time. They are all buried in the churchyard, but the Kellys have never gone in for ostentation in any way and there are no ornate tombstones, or memorials in the true sense. Kelly itself is their memorial.

There have been two Kellys of note outside their immediate locality. A Mary Kelly was very keen on amateur theatricals and staged local pageants to such a high standard that she took them on tour all over the country, including Stratford-upon-Avon, and much of her work is recorded in the Theatre Museum in London.

The second was Admiral Kelly, who by his will dated 29 September 1866 left the greater part of his real and personal estate to trustees founding a charity which he directed should be called 'The Kelly College'. The Founder's Day service held annually at Kelly College, built on the outskirts of Tavistock on land given by the Duke of Bedford for the purpose, begins with the reading of his will. Benedictus Marwood Kelly, was born in February 1785 in Holsworthy where his father was a surgeon. He entered the Navy in 1798 as a midshipman, spending much of his time with the Channel fleet until promoted to Lieutenant in 1805 when he sailed around the Cape of Good Hope, across to Jamaica and back to England in 1811 and promotion to Commander. In 1821 he was appointed Captain of HMS *Royal George*, aged thirty-six, but recurring ill health forced his early retirement shortly thereafter. However, in accordance with naval customs of the time, he was appointed to the Reserve List of Flag Officers, first as Rear Admiral, and in 1863 as Admiral by which time he was aged seventy-eight. His first wife, Mary Ann, died within a year of their marriage, and it seems that about this time the idea of founding a college was taking root, because it was recorded of him that he lived a 'most penurious life', in just one room in London where he had business interests as Director of the LB & SC Railway, and the Bristol & Exeter Railway, and also of the Royal Mail Steam Packet Company. In 1855 he married again, the daughter of a coalmine owner, and bought Saltford, an estate near Bath, situated on top of the Box tunnel. It was estimated by one relative that the amount he left for the founding of Kelly College was in the region of £132,000. Admiral Kelly's will set out in great detail how the college was to be run; the headmaster's salary, for example, was to be the equivalent of 'the value of 100 bushels of wheat during the year ending 30 December next'. The Admiral died in 1867, and was buried at Holsworthy. Kelly College opened five years later and has gone from strength to strength.

But the old house at Kelly has often served its purpose. Margery Kelly remembers it chock-a-block full of refugees during the war, as well as Kelly relations who found this quiet corner of Devon a safe haven. The house was also home to Polish and Canadian airmen recuperating, and it was not uncommon for them, once again airborne, to swoop over Kelly dropping off packages of chocolate and other luxuries. From time to time they still turn up to see the old place. When life returned more or less to normal, the Kellys made good use of their huge walled garden and for a long time it was a profitable market garden, but when the railway line down the Tamar Valley connecting them to the main line and their markets was axed, the enterprise ceased to be profitable, as was the case for every other market gardener in the area.

Kelly House and the Kellys face an uncertain future. Yet it seems a pity that so much history should be casually cast aside. This family and its home are so typical of many of the old families of Devon that have either disappeared or are fighting for survival. Must we only preserve the great houses of wealthy families, and, in some cases, the once poor (a certain Liverpudlian guitarist springs to mind) and leave the middle to disappear without trace? Not for nothing were they once dubbed the 'backbone of England'. They never failed to answer the call to duty; they deserve better of us.

*Michael Kelly, aged fourteen, painted by his brother Nicholas.*

Courtesy Kelly family

*Margery Kelly – staying on.*

Courtesy Kelly family

# LOPES *of Maristow*

## *Quod tibi id alii* – Do as you would be done by

The Lopes family are not at all typical of Devonshire gentry. They have been in Devon only since the early days of the nineteenth century, having originated in Jamaica; they were originally Jewish, and the first baronet spent two years in gaol for bribery. However, the second Lord Roborough served for twenty years as Lord Lieutenant and he and his wife were typical English country gentlefolk.

Mordecai Rodriguez Lopes was born in the London suburb of Clapham. He was of Spanish origins, and possibly the family came over with William of Orange, who had reason to be grateful to the Jewish community.

His wife, Rebecca, was the daughter of a wealthy Jamaican planter, Manasseh Perera, and their son, Manasseh Massey Lopes, was born in Jamaica in 1755. He was a colourful character and decided to come to England to make his fortune, which it would seem he achieved. In 1802 he entered Parliament, winning the seat of Romney, and that same year he 'abjured Judaism for the Church of England'. Lopes was created a baronet in 1805, (with a remainder to his nephew Ralph Franco) obtaining a Royal Licence to take the name of Massey before his own. In 1812 and '18 he was returned for Barnstaple, but he was later accused of laying out large sums in 'persauding' the electorate to the tune of £35 each. Whether he was guilty or not of the charge of bribery is a matter for conjecture, but in 1819 he was unseated on this charge, fined £1000 and spent two years in Exeter

*Maristow in its heyday.*

gaol. He returned in triumph to the House in 1823 as Member for Westbury, which he represented until his death, and was made Recorder of Westbury. In 1795 he had married Charlotte Yeates from Monmouth and three years later purchased the Maristow estate on the banks of the River Tamar, for the considerable sum of £65,000, including all its contents. When he died in 1831, it was rumoured he was worth £800,000, (over £33 million in today's terms), mainly in Government and East India stock, with which he had connections The actual proven sum was £170,000 with £45,000 duty paid.

Sir Manasseh left no children so the title and his estate duly passed to his nephew, son of his sister Esther Lopes, who had married Abraham Franco. Ralph Franco later changed his name to Lopes under the term of his uncle's will. Sir Ralph also 'inherited' the seat for Westbury, and was a JP for Wiltshire and Devon. He later represented South Devon in Parliament and married Susan Gibbs a member of the Ludlow family from Wiltshire.

They had five sons, the eldest of whom followed his father and grandfather into Parliament, the third member of his family to represent Westbury, which he took over on his father's death in 1854. Two brothers became barristers, one going on to become a QC and Recorder of Exeter, a High Court judge, then receiving a knighthood in 1876. Another, Henry, became first Baron Ludlow of Heywood.

Sir Massey Lopes, the third baronet, was an educated man, gaining an MA at Oxford. He was a respected politician, refusing Disraeli's offer of Chancellor of the Exchequer. Agriculture was a main interest and he spent much time and money improving his estates at Maristow. In Parliament he urged the grievance of local taxation which he saw imposed a burden on the labourers, and helped to pass the Agricultural Ratings Act. He was made a Privy Councillor, and was a Civil Lord of the Admiralty from 1874–80. He was High Sheriff for Devon and a JP and DL for both Devon and Wiltshire. His wife was Berthe Yarde-Buller, only daughter of the first Lord Churston.

*Sir Massey Lopes, 3rd Bt.*

Their son, Henry Yarde-Buller Lopes, became the fourth baronet in 1908. He studied history at Oxford, gaining an honours degree and was later called to the Bar. He twice unsuccessfully contested Devon seats, and was returned for Grantham in 1892, which he held until 1900. However, he was more interested in local politics and affairs, and was one of the first members of the newly formed Devon County Council, and its Chairman from 1916 until his death in 1938. He married in 1891 Lady Alberta, daughter of the Earl of Mount Edgcumbe. During their time, they spent generously on Maristow. The original sixteenth century house had been considerably enlarged and remodelled by successive owners – George III visited Maristow when he was staying at Saltram – and when Sir Massey bought the property it was described as a two-storey Palladian house. An estimated £16,000 was spent on deeper foundations, new cellars, floors, raising of the roof, and the installation of an electric light plant and electric wiring. Sir Henry was made the first Baron Roborough in January 1938 but died in April the same year.

*Sir Henry Lopes, 3rd Chairman of Devon County Council 1916–38.*

*The late Lord and Lady Roborough.*
Courtesy Lopes family

Massey Henry Edgcumbe Lopes, born in 1903, inherited as the second baron and devoted most of his long life to charitable and local affairs. Educated at Eton and Oxford, he served as ADC to the Governor General of South Africa before joining the Scots Guards at the outset of the Second World War, where he attained the rank of Major. He was also active locally, as Hon. Col of the Devon TA and of the Devon Army Cadet Force. Lord Roborough became the Vice Lieutenant of the county in 1951, and from 1958 until 1978 he held the position of Lord Lieutenant. He also served as a member of the Prince of Wales Council for ten years, and was a member of the committees of Dartmoor National Park and Devon's Outward Bound School. He married in 1936 Helen Dawson, who was a keen and knowledgeable gardener. They lived at Maristow until it was requisitioned during the war, and the family never lived in it again. Such was its condition upon its return, that Lord Roborough decided to lease it to the Church of England Board as a home for retired clergy. Only two years after the first arrivals and a considerable expenditure on bringing it up to date, fire seriously damaged the roof. The County Council took over the lease, carried out basic repairs and ran the house as a home for educationally sub-normal children for twenty years. They left in 1976 and for two years this lovely house stood empty until being taken over by an outward bound school. During their tenure the second fire occurred in 1982, followed by a third three months later. By now the house was devastated, and the Maristow Trustees, seeing no end in prospect, applied for permission to demolish. There was tremendous opposition, with two public inquiries and two refusals.

The final solution was a happy one and Maristow survived long enough to be turned into attractive homes by Kit Martin, a specialist in lost-cause houses. By the time he stepped in little was left except the shell; vandals had stripped the fireplaces and the staircases, and floors and ceilings had collapsed, but today the house looks once again as lovely as it must have done when George III and his family strolled on the terrace.

Lord Roborough had two sons, Henry Massey Lopes who succeeded as third baron in 1992, and George Lopes of Gnaton Hall. Henry married Robyn Bromwich from Australia (now divorced) and their eldest son is Massey John Henry, born in 1969.

# NORTHCOTE *of Iddesleigh*

## *Christi Crux est mea lux* – The cross of Christ of my Light

From Galfridus, known to be living at Northcote in 1103, down to Stafford, the fourth and present earl, the Northcotes stretch in unbroken male line. One of the present Lord Iddesleigh's most prized possessions is a very beautiful and very long scroll incorporating all the heraldic coats of arms, supporters, and devices of each successive head of the family, and their wives, who have added to their not inconsiderable holdings over the centuries.

By the early fourteenth century the family had moved from Northcote in the parish of East Down, near Barnstaple, to Newton St Cyres, and later that century John de Northcote was High Sheriff of the county. Several generations later John, of Crediton, married the daughter and heiress of Edmund Drew of Hayne, near Newton, which property has been in the family ever since. It was their son John who bought Upton and there he lived with his wife Elizabeth and their 12 sons and six daughters. The oldest of this enormous brood, also John, brought the family to prominence by becoming Sheriff in 1627and MP for Ashburton from 1640–60, which included the Long Parliament. In 1641 he was created a baronet. During the difficult years of the Civil War, Sir John managed to keep a low profile, despite having played host to Charles I at Hayne in 1644, and serving in the local militia. He saw action as a captain with the Earl of Stamford on the Cromwellian side, yet was returned to Parliament at the Restoration, which he appears to have supported, and where he remained until 1676.

The Northcotes were moving up in the world, and Sir Arthur, the next baronet, married the daughter of Sir Francis Godolphin the Lord High Treasurer. It was the fifth baronet, Sir Henry, who made the most advantageous marriage in terms of land, by marrying the heiress of his neighbour, Hugh Stafford of Pynes, in 1732. Hayne, until then their chief residence, sank to farmhouse status, and Sir Henry moved into the grand new house overlooking the River Exe, built by his father-in-law in the early 1700s. By Devon standards, Pynes is large, with over 60 rooms, and certainly imposing, and the family continued to live there until the 1990s.

*Galfridus – the first recorded Northcote.* Courtesy Earl of Iddesleigh

*Monument to Sir John Northcote 1570–1632 and his two wives in Newton St Cyres church.*

*Sir John Northcote, lst Bt.*
    Courtesy Earl of Iddesleigh

*The first Earl of Iddesleigh, Stafford Northcote.*    Courtesy Earl of Iddesleigh

*Pynes, lived in by the family from the 1700s until the 1990s.*

The Stafford family also owned much of the village of Iddesleigh in mid Devon from which the Northcotes take their title, and although they still have the village green and the Lordship of the Manor, the rest was sold off in the early 1900s by Walter the second earl, though apparently it was his dishonest agent who benefited rather more than the earl.

Stafford Henry (b.1818), the best known member of the family, was the grandson of the seventh baronet and his wife, a daughter of Charles Baring, Lord Northbrook. He had a distinguished political career, entering Parliament as MP for Dudley in 1855. He represented North Devon from 1866 until his retirement in 1885. During that time he served first as Private Secretary to Gladstone who was President of the Board of Trade, becoming President himself in 1866; Secretary of State for India in 1867, Chancellor of the Exchequer and Leader of the House of Commons from 1874–80, and First Lord of the Treasury from 1885–86. By all accounts he was a charming and popular man, not an easy achievement for a politician, and when his elevation to the peerage was under discussion, the story goes that Queen Victoria, with whom he was a special favourite, waived away the rank of viscount, usually bestowed in such circumstances, and declared he should become an earl outright 'because he had such beautiful manners'. The earldom was bestowed upon him in 1885, and the next year he was appointed Lord Lieutenant. He died in 1887. The first earl took a great interest in a reform school for 'bad boys from the towns' which he built on the estate, the first of its kind in the country. He used to go over and check progress at weekends. The building was later turned into four cottages, known as Reformatory Cottages, which survived until recent times, when they were reluctantly bulldozed as being uneconomic to modernise being totally without any amenities and in the middle of a field.

His political spark passed to his second son, Henry, who entered the Foreign Office in 1868. He was active in various joint High Commissions, one in Washington to consider relations between Great Britain and the USA, and later joined the Diplomatic Service. He was Private Secretary to the Chancellor of the Exchequer until he resigned in 1880 to stand successfully for Parliament as member for Exeter. Henry Northcote became a baronet in 1887 and Baron Northcote of the City of Exeter in 1900 in which year he was appointed Governor of Bombay. His last political appointment was as Governor General of Australia from 1903–08 and as a result he carried the Standard of Australia at the coronation of George V. He died in 1911 without children.

John, his younger brother, followed several of his forebears and entered the Church. He rose from being vicar of St Andrew's, Westminster to become Hon. Chaplain to both Queen Victoria and Edward VII, and it was his son who became the third earl.

A fourth brother, Arthur, also entered the Church and became a Canon of Bury St Edmunds, marrying three times and having five daughters and one son, Sir Geoffrey. The latter also had a distinguished diplomatic career, mainly in Africa where in 1948 he became the first Speaker of the East Africa Legislature, and ended his career as Governor of Hong Kong.

*Walter, 2nd Earl of Iddesleigh.*

Walter, the second earl, served as Chairman of the Board of the Inland Revenue. As his only son died a year before him in 1926 without issue, the title went to his nephew Henry Stafford, and Pynes and all his estates to his unmarried daughter Rosalind. Henry, in the eyes of his uncle, had committed the sin of converting to Catholicism, and although Rosalind willed the estates back to him, the family tiara was left directly to Henry's wife.

Rosalind lived for quarter of a century in Pynes. She had a great affection for the place, but no formal training in estate matters, yet insisted on managing it all herself. She had to contend with the depression of the 1930s and the Second World War, during which time Pynes was requisitioned by the Ministry of Works. She became increasingly frail and spent less and less time outside. The estate was later managed by an Exeter solicitor. When Henry, known to all as Harry, eventually gained possession following Rosalind's death in 1950, he found a house riddled with dry rot, dilapidated and unmodernised. In an attempt to make it economic, he converted part into several flats occupying the two wings of the William and Mary block. This was done partly to keep all of the house occupied, partly so that someone would tell him when the roof was leaking as he never had time to check all the attics after it had rained, and partly to try to help solve the housing shortage as he had a great social conscience. He also inherited much of the village of Upton Pyne, with 54 cottages and only one WC between them! He was so embarrassed that he sold most of them off, mainly to the existing tenants for next to nothing, and in 1957 passed the estate over to his son, Stafford, the present earl. The third earl took a keen interest in the House of Lords, where he sat on the cross-benches for forty-three years. His wife remained at Pynes until her death in 1991.

*The 3rd Earl and Countess of Iddesleigh in coronation robes.*
Courtesy Earl of Iddesleigh

Pynes was never the childhood or family home of Stafford, fourth Lord Iddesleigh and on the death of his mother in 1991, the house passed to her grandson John, the present Viscount St Cyres, who preferred to live in the older and more manageable property at Hayne. Lord St Cyres eventually sold it following his divorce.

Lord Iddesleigh built for himself a modern 'stately home' on the outskirts of the village, where the ancestral portraits of the Northcotes and the Staffords stare down from the walls. Lord Iddesleigh is a man of many interests, serving as a district councillor for many years until politics crept in, at which point he retired. His National Service was spent in the Irish

Guards and he has lasting memories of mounting guard at the lying-in-state of George VI and of lining the route for the funeral. He has been involved with the Devon and Exeter Steeplechases, local television and radio companies and was Chairman of the Trustee Savings Bank in the days 'when we set the interest rates before the government took over'. For many years Lord Iddesleigh also chaired Upton Pyne Parish Council and has served with the British Legion, the CLA and the Devon Agricultural Association. He remembers that his maiden speech in the House of Lords, which he occasionally attended, was on 'The Problems of the West Country'.

He has been a Deputy Lieutenant since 1979 and is currently Vice Lord Lieutenant, which means he finds himself standing in for the Lord Lieutenant at all sorts of ceremonies and functions. Lord Iddesleigh has retired from many of his chairmanships and finds plenty to do running the estate, with the help of his son who farms the 2000 or so acres around Upton Pyne and Hayne, which include a large percentage of forestry. Lady Iddesleigh was Maria Luisa Alvarez-Builla, Condesa del Real Agrado of Spain, and her mother was the widow of Viscount Exmouth. Mima, as she is known, was awarded the OBE in 1988 for her services over many years to the British Red Cross and for her voluntary work over many years in the county. In 1987 Lady Iddesleigh was appointed a Deputy Lieutenant, making them the first husband and wife DLs in Devon.

*The 4th and present Earl and Countess of Iddesleigh celebrating the millennium in the village of Upton Pyne.*

Courtesy Earl of Iddesleigh

# PARKER *of Saltram*

## *Fideli certa merces* – Reward is sure to be faithful

The Parkers have lived at Saltram, described as the most beautiful house in the West Country, since the middle of the eighteenth century, but they originated in the north of the county. Their home was at North Molton on the edge of Exmoor where they are first mentioned in 1320. In the early sixteenth century Thomas Parker, a wool merchant, was the richest man in the parish and it is possible that a wool-stapler's mark still to be seen in the village was his. It does seem to contain the letters T and P and the building would have been much more than a humble cottage in Tudor times. Certainly the Parkers went on to build a small manor house across the square, adjoining the church – the Bampfyldes lived on the other side – and several of them were buried there. Thomas Parker, who died in 1566, was the last to live at North Molton for it was his elder son, John, who moved south to become the tenant of Boringdon, near Plympton. His grandson, also John, consolidated the family's position by marrying Frances, daughter and heiress of Jeronomy Mayhew, owner of the Boringdon estate. In due course, their son Edmund, born 1593, inherited both Boringdon and the North Molton estates, and raised the family profile by marrying Amy Seymour, daughter of Sir Edward Seymour of Berry Pomeroy. Their grandson, George, served as High Sherriff, and as MP for Plymouth from 1695–98. He married twice, firstly to Elizabeth Fowell, from nearby Fowelscombe, and secondly Anne Buller from Morval, and it was with their son, John, born in 1703, that the story of the Parkers and Saltram can be said to begin.

George Parker added considerably to the family's lands during his lifetime. The Whiteway estate near Chudleigh was purchased in 1724, and the Polsloe Priory lands at Exeter a decade or so later, but it was the purchase of the Saltram estate from Sir George Carteret in 1712 that was to have the greatest effect on the family. At that time it was tenanted out, and it may be that George and his family had no wish to leave Boringdon, which over the centuries had been considerably extended and altered. One lasting improvement, however, was carried out by George Parker; he enclosed the house in the midst of 220 acres of deer park, for which a royal licence was required, and which ensured the protection and privacy of Saltram. Before he could make any further plans, George Parker died in 1743.

*Boringdon House, c.1809.*

*Wool sign in North Molton.*

*Saltram House c. 1832.*

It seemed that John and his grand wife, Lady Catherine, daughter of the first Earl Poulett, Lord Steward to Queen Anne, were intent on remaining at Boringdon, for William Kent was asked to prepare designs for a grand new house. These were never implemented. Neither was the grandiose scheme for a new house at Saltram with a 370-foot facade, bearing a resemblance to the Fortescue house at Castle Hill. When this was drawn up is not known, but Lady Catherine seems first to have contemplated moving to Saltram when her husband fell seriously ill, planning to build herself a dower house there. But he recovered and the decision was made to move to Saltram. It was at this time that the existing house was adapted and enlarged with a new south front and a linking block.

Lady Catherine was the moving force behind the rebuilding of Saltram. The modest house suddenly doubled in size and the interior was lavishly decorated with rococo plasterwork in all the principal rooms, while the grounds were laid out much as they are today. In her lifetime, Saltram was already becoming well known for its style and beauty. Lady Catherine died in 1758.

It was said that when her husband died ten years later, 135 bags of money containing £29,973 15s 2d were found hidden around the house, the whereabouts and exact contents of each meticulously noted. Their elder surviving son, John, inherited Saltram and Boringdon whilst the younger brother, Montagu, moved to the Whiteway estates. Three generations later the estates were again united when Montagu's great-granddaughter Harriet married her cousin Edmund, second Earl of Morley.

John Parker moved in court circles and in 1784, George III ennobled John as Baron Boringdon. He had followed a political career, serving as an MP for twenty-three years from 1761, and his other great interest was horse racing. He spent lavishly on his stables and in 1783 his stud produced a Derby winner, named Saltram. When his financial difficulties forced him to sell up, the Prince of Wales was amongst the purchasers.

It is to this man and his beautiful wife, Theresa Robinson, that we owe the magnificent Adam interiors of Saltram. The Georgian heyday produced many fine houses throughout the country, and at Saltram there is a wonderful example of this age of elegance, considered pre-eminent even then. The Parkers commissioned portraits from the foremost artists, in particular, Sir Joshua Reynolds, a close friend who was born and raised at nearby Plympton. However, also in common with many of his contemporaries, Lord Boringdon's ideas outweighed his income, and Adam's grand scheme for rebuilding the north wing with a 71ft gallery was never implemented. When he died in 1788, he left an estate encumbered with £58,000 of debt. His son, who was only sixteen, lived for a time with his uncle in Yorkshire and Saltram was let out, first to the Marquess of Lansdowne who had been a great friend of his father, and later George III and his retinue chose Saltram for a stay in the West Country.

John, second Lord Boringdon, entered Parliament at an early age, and left his aunt to run Saltram. He married twice, divorcing his first wife, Augusta, daughter of the Earl of Westmorland in 1809. Their eleven-year old son died in 1817 so that it was Edmund, son of his second wife, Frances Talbot, who eventually inherited. He served with the North Devon Militia, appointed Colonel in 1799, and was responsible for the defence of part of the south coast against possible invasion. Edmund was created Earl of Morley in 1815, and made a few modest improvements to the house, but what ran away with his money was the ambitious land drainage scheme at Chelson Meadow below the house. This is thought to have cost in the region of £15,000, for which a mortgage on the estate was needed. A race-course was laid out on the reclaimed land, and in 1825 a bridge was constructed to cross the river and provide a new quick route into Plymouth. This brought an income of £700 per annum in tolls, and remained in use until replaced in 1961. With his lifestyle and ambitious schemes, the first earl had run up debts totalling £258,000 by the time he died in 1840.

The second earl did his best to tow the family out of its financial crisis, but only made matters worse when he decided to form a china clay company at Lee Moor. Far from helping, it proved a disaster and finally crashed in 1861. The earl sold his London house, and Saltram was let with the family moving to Whiteway. On his death three years later, matters were so bad that there was no succession duty to pay as it was considered that the liabilities of the estate outweighed its worth. (Albert) Edmund Parker, third Lord Morley, took out a mortgage of £23,000 and insured his own life for £5000.

Following family tradition, Lord Morley joined the Liberals under Gladstone and served as Lord-in-Waiting to Queen Victoria. He became Under-Secretary for War in 1880 and was instrumental in sorting out the Suez Canal problems. He was a Privy Councillor and from 1889 until his death in 1905 he was Chairman of Committees of the House of Lords. In Devon this energetic man served his county first as Chairman of the Quarter Sessions until 1880 and when this was replaced by Devon County Council, he was firstly Vice-chairman and then Chairman.

*Albert Edmund Parker, 3rd Earl of Morley.*

There was no spare money for doing anything other than maintenance work at Saltram, which was in a poor state when the family returned to live there in 1884. A major problem had been the drainage; two large cesspits constructed in the cellars below the grand Adam saloon were served by soil pipes which had completely rotted through. Substantial sums were raised by selling off some of the Reynolds and Van Dyke portraits. Lord Morley negotiated a favourable deal with the railway company which wanted to make use of the Laira embankment and the new bridge, guaranteeing him £1450 a year in tolls, pontage for use of the bridge up to £8000 a year and £5000 worth of ordinary shares in the company. But the sale of Saltram was only staived off by a loan from his step-uncle. The future of the estate was at last assured when Edmund married Margaret Holford, from Westonbirt in Gloucestershire. Together they set about repairing and restoring the house. Of their three sons, Edmund and Montagu succeeded as fourth and fifth earls respectively, but as neither married, it is the son of John (Jack), the youngest son, who is the present earl. May, their only sister, who had married Lionel St Aubyn in 1915, continued to live at Saltram with her husband and children, running the household until her untimely death in 1932, aged fifty.

The two brothers were something of an oddity. The fourth earl always known as 'B' for Boringdon, lived on at Saltram, becoming increasingly reclusive. The Whiteway estate was sold off in the 1920s, and the Holford inheritance of Westonbirt and Dorchester House in London was also sold, although he kept the famous Westonbirt Arboretum which was a consuming interest. He spent one week in four there and it is thought he planted more trees than anyone else.

Montagu nearly came to a premature end in the Holy Land. In 1908 he became part of an expedition to discover the whereabouts of the Ark of the Covenant. This took a great deal of money to finance, and seems to have been as much a treasure hunt as a serious archeological dig, apparently undertaken without the knowledge of the proper authorities. They were incensed when they discovered what was going on, and the expedition had to flee for their lives. A great deal of British diplomacy was required to soothe things down. These two bachelor brothers lived through the Second World War at Saltram, mounting a guard on the roof to watch out for incendiaries, which were promptly swept off. The fourth earl died in 1951, and his brother succeeded. To safeguard Saltram and the estate he negotiated a deal with the Treasury that they would accept the house and contents in lieu of death duties The Treasury passed them over to the National Trust who kept a watching brief until 1962 when the fifth earl died.

These were difficult years for the Parkers. John (Jack) Parker, the youngest of the three brothers, had married Marjory Katherine St Aubyn from St Michael's Mount in Cornwall and at no stage had they been consulted or informed of the future plans for Saltram. They watched with some dismay the growing friendship of a certain lady with the fifth earl and it is recorded in the family diary that when he died, leaving everything to her, some £58,000, 'MKP was much put out'. When the National Trust at last took over, a three-day sale was held at Saltram in 1964 of surplus furniture no longer required by the Trust, and although Marjory Parker did her best, paying £2 10s for a lot of Frances, Lady Morley's drawings and books and buying a further set of seven paintings, the family did not get all they had hoped for.

Jack Parker with a wife and family to support, needed a job. On leaving Cambridge, he had gone to Canada and helped build a railway in Alaska and then worked on other railway projects in Canada and America. During the war he was a railway sapper, so it seemed natural that he should take up a position as Assistant Development Agent with the Great Western Railway, which took him away from home a great deal. In 1932 the family moved to Plymouth and moved into their present home at Pound, near Yelverton. Diaries kept by the family record young John (the present earl) being sent home from Eton in 1939 because of a shortage of gas masks, and his brother in 1947 because the Thames came up the drains. The family were evacuated from Pound when the house was requisitioned and an airfield was created on Roborough Down. After the war German prisoners-of-war were housed in the wartime buildings there, and Lord Morley's father, who had retired from the GWR, employed them clearing the woodland around the house, paying them in cigarettes.

John Parker followed most of his family to Eton. From there he went straight into the Army and the Second World War. In 1955 he married Johanna Molesworth St Aubyn from Pencarrow in Cornwall, and they held their reception at Londonderry House, one of the last glittering social gatherings before its demolition. In August the following year he was recalled from leave because of the Suez crisis, leaving home just before the birth of his first son. He became a Lieutenant Colonel with the Royal Fusiliers and served in North-West Europe, Palestine, Korea and the Sudan, before retiring in 1970. He did not lose all his links with the military way of life as he was made an Hon. Col of the Devon ACF and of the fourth Btn Devon & Dorset TA regiment. Compared with the activity and variety of his life since leaving the Army, he must look back on his service days as something of a haven of peace.

Lord Morley immediately became involved in farming, running Farm Industries Ltd. In 1972 he became a JP, and a year earlier he had accepted the first of many presidencies, that of the Plymouth Chamber of Trade. This was followed by the Chambers of Trade for Devon and Cornwall, and the West Country Tourist Board He has been a governor of Plymouth Polytechnic and of Seale Hayne Agricultural College, and served on the Devon and Cornwall Regional Committee of the National Trust from 1969 to 1984. All these were, of course, voluntary appointments unlike his regional chairmanship of Lloyds Bank, where he remained on the Board until 1989. Lord Morley will be best remembered, however, for his long spell as Lord Lieutenant of the county. He served a long apprenticeship, first as DL from 1973–78, then as Vice Lord Lieutenant until 1982, and thereafter he conscientiously and with great energy, fulfilled his numerous duties all over the county. Throughout most of their married life, Lady Morley has accompanied her husband, to their various overseas postings, and then on his many official duties. Her own list of commitments is formidable: she has been Patron of the Devon Guides, President of the League of Friends of the Royal Eye Infirmary, President of the West of England School for Children with Little Sight, she is involved with the Children's Hospice South West, the Red Cross, St Luke's and the Drink and Drugs refuge – but she says hers has been largely a supporting role.

Their son, Mark, followed his father into the Army but now works for the John Lewis Partnership, and their daughter Venetia, having written a thesis on the future of the Upper House, now works there in the library.

*Lord Morley as Lord Lieutenant with Lady Morley.* Courtesy Earl of Morley

$\diamond\diamond\blacklozenge\diamond\diamond$

# PELLEW *of Canonteign*

*Deo Adjuvante* – God being my helper

The Pellews are a Cornish family, with Norman origins. Sometime before the seventeenth century, they left Breage and took to seafaring, one ancestor settling near Plymouth and another at Treverry near Falmouth. By the end of the century, Humphrey Pellew had amassed sufficient wealth to retire from the sea and continued to prosper as a shipowner, merchant and owner of a Maryland plantation. Humphrey combined with Samuel Trefusis of Mylor, MP for Penryn, and together they developed the village of Flushing, at the same time as the Killigrews were developing Falmouth. The partnership between the two men was further cemented when Humphrey's son Israel, married Samuel's daughter, Gertrude Trefusis, at that time heiress to the Trefusis estates. All must have seemed set fair for a prosperous future but things went sadly wrong. Gertrude ceased to be the heiress, and by the time Humphrey died in 1721, somehow the family wealth had disappeared. Of Humphrey's family of six, only the youngest son, Samuel, had any children. He was only eight when his father died and as soon as he was old enough, Samuel went to sea with the Falmouth Packet Service. He later transferred to Dover, where he died in 1765, leaving a young family of six, the second son being Edward Pellew, born in 1757. His mother remarried, and Edward went to to live with his grandmother in her tiny cottage in Penzance. But he was still a member of the Trefusis family and could count on support from such prominent people as Lord Falmouth and Admiral Boscawen.

A seafaring career was inevitable for young Edward and with the threat of war in the Falklands in 1770, young Edward found himself aboard HMS *Juno* bound for what Dr Johnson described as 'a few spots of earth that were worthless'. Edward Pellew's rise in the Navy was meteoric, but this was an era of great naval activity when a seaman of capabilities could make his way up to the very highest positions, which is what Edward Pellew did. His next expedition was under Captain Pownoll when in 1776 he sailed for Canada and the St Lawrence river.

Promotion at that time depended very much on patronage, and with a Whig government in power, a Tory such as Pellew could look for little favour, so on his return from Canada a spell ashore followed. In 1783 he married Susan, the daughter of a Wiltshire squire. 'I roused my wife out of a snug corner in a little retired village before she had ever heard a gun or seen the sea,' he said, but she appears to have adapted very well to the life of a naval officer's wife. The Boscawen patronage secured for him the parliamentary seat of Truro, where he was appointed an alderman and a magistrate, and for a while the Pellews lived at Flushing. But with a change in government, Captain Pellew was soon back at sea, bound for Newfoundland. His first major sea battle was in 1793 when his ship, the *Nymphe*, overcame and captured a French man-of-war. Later that year he was introduced by Lord Chatham to George III who conferred upon him a knighthood, followed by a baronetcy in 1796, bestowed in recognition of his part in rescuing the troops and crew of the *Dutton*. This was an amazing and heroic action for Pellew at the time was ashore, on his way to Plymouth with his wife, when he was told of the wreck of the *Dutton*, a Dutch East Indiaman full of troops, under the Citadel. Sir Edward hastened to the scene and soon took charge, rigging up rescue ropes to haul those on board to the shore. Calling for a volunteer to go aboard to rally the crew, he received no answer so he went himself, quickly rigging up two further sets of ropes, and standing guard whilst the women and children embarked in the ship's rowing boats to be rescued by a sloop that was standing by. Pellew did not leave the stricken ship until all were saved.

*Admiral Pellew, the 1st Viscount Exmouth.*

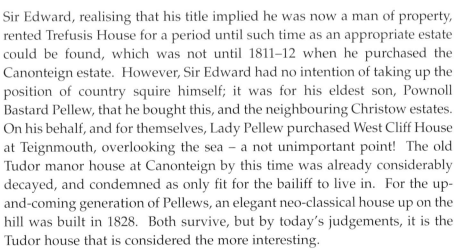

*Canonteign House.*

Sir Edward, realising that his title implied he was now a man of property, rented Trefusis House for a period until such time as an appropriate estate could be found, which was not until 1811–12 when he purchased the Canonteign estate. However, Sir Edward had no intention of taking up the position of country squire himself; it was for his eldest son, Pownoll Bastard Pellew, that he bought this, and the neighbouring Christow estates. On his behalf, and for themselves, Lady Pellew purchased West Cliff House at Teignmouth, overlooking the sea – a not unimportant point! The old Tudor manor house at Canonteign by this time was already considerably decayed, and condemned as only fit for the bailiff to live in. For the up-and-coming generation of Pellews, an elegant neo-classical house up on the hill was built in 1828. Both survive, but by today's judgements, it is the Tudor house that is considered the more interesting.

Five unproductive and unhappy years followed as C in C of the East Indies and it was with much relief that he hastened home to take up a position as

Commander in Chief of the North Sea, quickly followed by Command of the Mediterranean Fleet in 1811, whose principal task was one of blockading the French. A description of those last days of traditional ships of the line recalls their majesty and beauty:

*The British Mediterranean Fleet under Sir Edward Pellew, now Lord Exmouth, was anchored not far from us, and it was impossible to witness a more splendid naval armament. Together with several seventy-fours and frigates, there were five immense three-deckers; the port was constantly covered with small vessels and boats exhibiting a scene of the utmost animation; music seemed to be the principal source of amusement on board the English fleet. The morning and evening gun, accompanied by a volley of musketry from each ship, produced a grand effect, when echoed through the surrounding heights, though it might not have been so welcome to some drowsy listeners. Besides the reveille played by drums and fifes, at day-light, there was a military symphony every evening after sunset; this performed in reciprocal responses by the different ships, and associated with a serene sky, and the stillness of the sea, really seemed to partake of magical illusion.*

Pellew, who had been a Vice Admiral for some years, was appointed Admiral of the Blue in 1814, quickly followed by elevation to the peerage as Baron Exmouth. With Napoleon's escape from Elba and the commencement of the Hundred Days War, Lord Exmouth found himself recalled to command the Mediterranean Fleet. Once this excitement was over and Boney safely secure on St Helena, Lord Exmouth was given his final task, which brought him considerable fame. The Barbary States – the Mediterranean fringe of North Africa – had proved of great use as safe anchorage and source of supplies during the French Wars, and it was now time to conclude certain treaties with them. Piracy was rife, and one of the less favourable aspects was the imprisonment and enslavement of the seamen captured, most of them Christian. Exmouth manoeuvred his fleet outside Algiers and prepared to negotiate. He successfully ransomed over 400 slaves, mainly from the Italian coasts, but this still left 700 in captivity. He moved to Tunisia, rescuing a further 524, so far without a shot being fired, to the considerable regret of some of the crew! The fleet sailed for Gibraltar and it was whilst there that the news of the massacre of 200 simple coral fishermen whilst on shore hearing Mass, reached Lord Exmouth. Although it is probable that this was caused by a breakdown in communications between the Turkish overlords and their troops, Lord Exmouth's response was swift and he set sail for Algiers. There followed a spectacular action with the fleet bombarding the harbour and defences, bringing their vessels 'so close they could see the enemies' faces, their eyes and the frowning muzzles of their guns'. The Turkish fleet was completely destroyed, and much of the harbour. At the conclusion of hostilities, Exmouth ordered that no man should rest until all the wounded had been tended, and then proceeded to give a great dinner, which he had ordered before the commencement of battle, 'when the health of all the officers was drunk, and then his Lordship's health, after which every body went to sleep, almost like dead men.'

As a result of this, 1083 slaves were liberated and a treaty signed that no Christians would be enslaved in the future. But Exmouth was saddened at what he considered heavy losses, 883 men out of a total of 6500. The Battle of Algiers ranks as one of the greatest sea battles; in no other action did ships empty their magazines and few lasted as long, with pandemonium for nine hours on end and more than 50,000 rounds fired. The losses were sixteen per cent whilst at Trafalgar they were only nine per cent. Exmouth was considered by many to be the greatest sea officer of his time, and had he not been overshadowed by Nelson, with whom he never served, his fame would have been the greater. Lord Exmouth 'struck his flag' on 8 October 1816 and never went to sea again. He was fifty-nine.

His reward was a viscountcy, and numerous honours. In retirement, Lord Exmouth regularly attended the House of Lords, a strong supporter of the Duke of Wellington except on the Catholic question, and his final honour was to be made Vice Admiral of England. In January 1833 he died and was buried in Christow church, 'a church he had hardly known near that country house in which he had never lived'. The booming of the guns at Plymouth marked his passing.

Displayed in the church is, or was, the flag that flew from his ship at the Battle of Algiers, 'rescued from the great fire at the Arsenal, Devonport in 1840 and restored to the family by Mr Lumsdale, RNM Attendant at the Dockyard, who was Master of the Flagship during the Battle'.

In the one-hundred-and-thirty-seven years since 1833, until the tenth viscount inherited in 1970, there have been nine viscounts. The first Lord Exmouth had a large family of four sons and two daughters, and from three of those four sons a viscount descended.

Pownoll, the second viscount (who died in the same year as his father), married twice and the third and fourth viscounts were both his sons, but half-brothers. His first wife, whom he married in Bengal, was Eliza, daughter of Sir George Barlow, whom he later divorced. His second wife was Georgiana, daughter of Mungo Dick.

*Edward, 5th viscount.*

Pownoll followed his father into the Navy, but did not rise above the rank of captain. It was, after all, a time of peace and little naval activity, and the old system of promotion no longer applied. Younger sons saw foreign service. Pownoll's second son served in India and died in 1848. Pownoll's youngest son died in 1866 at the age of thirty-six, and another son died on Christmas Day 1851 at Portsmouth after a short illness, aged twenty-eight. The walls of Christow church are lined with memorials to the Pellews including one to Sir Fleetwood Broughton Reynold Pellew, second son of Edward Viscount Exmouth, Admiral of the Blue, Companion of the Bath, who died in 1861 in Marseilles, and was buried in Florence.

The fifth viscount, Edward, died unmarried in 1922 at the age of thirty-two of an illness contracted serving in the Great War and the title passed to his cousin, Henry Edward, the son of George, the Very Reverend Dean of

*The present Viscount Exmouth.*

Norwich, and Prebendary of York, who became the sixth viscount. He had spent most of his life in America, and within six months he, too, died. His first wife was the daughter of Judge Jay of New York, and on her death he married her younger sister. Their son, Charles, was brought up an American. He fought in the Spanish-American war and was a member of the American Federation of Artillery and a Fellow of the Chemical Society, marrying the daughter of a New York professor. He did not take up UK citizenship until 1931. He married twice, but had only one daughter who shared the fate of several of her female ancestors and died unmarried in Paris in 1928 aged thirty-nine. The seventh viscount had five sisters, and died in 1945 when this line of descent also died.

The first viscount's fourth son, also Edward, was a clergyman and it was his grandson, Edward Irving, who inherited as eighth viscount in 1945. He was an army surgeon, and died in 1951. His only son, the ninth viscount, married the daughter of a Spanish grandee, Maria Louisa, the Marquesa de Olias, and it is their son who is the present viscount, inheriting in 1970, and who also married a wife of noble Spanish birth, Maria Krystina. His heir, Edward, born in 1978, is the son of his second wife Rosemary Scoones.

Lord Exmouth stood in the 2000 general election as a candidate for the UKIP party and, had he been elected, he would have been the first elected peer to sit in the House of Commons.

# QUICKE *of Newton St Cyres*

The Quickes are a quiet, unflamboyant lot, as Sir John puts it; they have never produced a famous general, admiral, leading politician or lawyer, or made their mark as courtiers. They have never been given, or sought, a title or high position. In consequence, few people outside their own county are aware of this charming and fascinating family who have quietly looked after their own acres since the days of the first Elizabeth.

Their early origins are uncertain, but it is thought that they are one of only a handful of county families who did not come over with the Conqueror, but are of Anglo-Saxon stock. They may have descended from a prominent tribe called the Hwicki in the Worcestershire area. The first certain knowledge of them is as Somerset farmers; the first John, and there have been ten of them as head of the family, owned land at West Monkton and at Sandford in the mid-fifteenth century. His son, Richard married the daughter of Thomas Bidewell of Bidwell-in-Newton, a farm that still exists, and it was their son Andrew who is first described as being of Newton St Cyres. At that time the parish was owned partly by the Quickes and partly by the Northcotes of Hayne, and it was not until the Reformation that they managed to gain possession of the entire manor which may have been the reason for Elizabeth I granting Arms to the Quickes in 1573.

The family seem to have made a point of not taking part in any of the affairs of state. There is no record of them at Agincourt, or of them fighting for either York or Lancaster; they stayed away. Even more remarkably they managed not to take sides in the Civil War, and avoided involvement with the rebels in the Western Rebellion of 1549.

By the mid-seventeenth century they were considered of sufficient importance for Andrew Quicke to marry the daughter of his neighbour, Sir Arthur Northcote of Hayne, who was married to a sister of the Lord Treasurer Godolphin. This gave them a strong connection with the Churchill family as Godolphin's son married Henrietta Churchill, who became Duchess of Marlborough in her own right. Thus the Quickes and the Churchills were cousins until Henrietta's line died out in 1731. Andrew died in 1736 and was succeeded by John the fifth, whose wife Rebecca was the heiress of Richard Nutcombe from Ashbrittle, an ancient family dating

*Monument to John Quicke in Newton St Cyres church.*

back to the thirteenth century. The couple had two sons: John who would inherit from his father, and Nutcombe, who was a clergyman and presented to the family living at Ashbrittle, but he preferred life at Exeter where he became Chancellor of the Cathedral, and married the Bishop's daughter, Anne Lavington. His mother ensured that her inheritance went to her second son, Nutcombe, who had two daughters.

The Quicke lands passed to John and Rebecca's grandson, John the sixth, as his father had died in 1729. He was the first Quicke to become High Sheriff in 1757, an honour also held by his son, also John (the seventh), in 1782. The Quickes by now were a family of some standing outside Devon and were no longer marrying the daughters of local families; John the seventh's mother had been the daughter of a wealthy Bristol merchant and MP, Thomas Coster, and he himself married into the Scottish Cumming family. His wife, Emilia Penrose Cumming, was the daughter of Grace Pearce, heiress to her uncle, John Penrose, of Penrose in Cornwall, and Alexander Cumming from Forres, in Morayshire. Emilia's brother was heir to his cousin, Sir William Gordon of Gordonstoun and in 1804 became Sir William Gordon-Cumming, when he sold the Penrose estate. And it was his descendant who was implicated in the notorious Tranby Croft baccarat scandal in the 1890s, losing his social position and retiring to his Scottish estates.

John and Emilia had a large family. Their second son Andrew became the vicar of Ashbrittle and persuaded his brother to enlarge considerably the vicarage and provide good stabling as he proposed to hunt. Edward became a Fellow of New College, Oxford and died unmarried; the next son, William, later took over as rector of Ashbrittle, and two other sons, Thomas and George, gained honour in the Napoleonic Wars, taking part in the Battle of Waterloo as captains in the King's Dragoon Guards. There was great rejoicing in Newton St Cyres when they both returned unharmed.

Newton House was a grand and large Georgian-style house built around a central courtyard but John Quicke had long objected to his view being

*Newton House after the fire in 1906.*
Courtesy Quicke family.

marred by the traffic on the road from Crediton to Exeter. To provide employment for returning soldiers, he used them to dig a 50ft-deep cutting between the house and the church and rerouted the road, building himself a bridge to reach the church.

The next John (the eighth) was more prominent in county affairs, becoming both a JP and DL, and High Sheriff in 1833. His wife was also a Cumming, Francis, daughter of Captain Thomas Cumming from Somerset and presumably a descendant of Alexander of Penrose. They had a large family of seven sons and three daughters. The Quicke estates by this time were extensive with lands in Newton St Cyres, Sandford, Shobrooke, Morchard Bishop, Crediton, North Tawton, Budleigh Salterton and Ashbrittle. However, John the eighth left a somewhat unusual will, and his decision to leave his many children £10,000 each caused the sale of thousands of acres to provide the money. There was also a clause that the estates would revert to his second son Thomas in the event of John his eldest son failing to produce an heir. This will was made a year after Thomas reached his majority in 1838, and ten years before the thirty-one-year-old John eventually married Mary Gould; there were no children. Thomas was a Fellow of Trinity College, Cambridge, and at that time it was still a requirement that a Fellow resigned should he marry. He died, unmarried, before his elder brother so that it was eventually the grandchildren of the next brother, the Revd Edward, vicar of Newton, who inherited in turn.

*Ernest Quicke.* Courtesy Quicke family

*Adelaide Quicke.*
Courtesy Quicke family

John the ninth who died in 1900 at the ripe old age of eighty-four was sufficiently prominent to serve both as a JP and DL, and as High Sheriff, but he was not popular and had a reputation for eccentricity. A shooting guest was banned from Newton for seven years because he had thrown his cigarette end onto the terrace; he was quite capable of pouring a jug of water over his wife if he did not like her dress, and on one occasion he decided to teach a lesson to a pushy undertaker who had turned up one evening after a bereavement on the estate. John Quicke lured him onto the bridge to cross to the church, but closed the gate in the poor man's face and locked it, whilst the butler was quietly locking the other end, and there he stayed all night. His long life spanned almost the whole of the nineteenth century, and he saw his income from his rich farm lands fall from the heights of the early years to the depths caused by the agricultural depression of the middle years. The repeal of the Corn Laws in 1872, which had the effect of splitting the Tory Party, started the downward spiral which accelerated after the Canadian Pacific Railway opened up the vast prairie lands of middle America and Canada causing cheap wheat to flood into the country. 'So Uncle John, who was accustomed to living like a prince, sold land to maintain his lifestyle.' Before this the estates had stood at around 10,000 acres in Devon and Dorset; all that now remains is the immediate estate of some 2400 acres. Until Thomas's death, John Quicke had regarded him as his heir, but on his death, perhaps because of the way he had been treated, he was unable to make up his mind, although the obvious successor was Ernest, the son of Edward. But Ernest, too, 'suffered from a somewhat riotous lifestyle' and having joined a cavalry regiment, got himself into debt, which was not unusual for young officers, but his kindly colonel

*Edward Quicke, killed in action*
Courtesy Quicke family

declined to come to the rescue a second time, and Ernest was sent off to New Zealand. There he married Adelaide, whose father, Arthur Collyns, had originated from Exmouth, and there their two sons, Edward and Noel, and a daughter Gladys, were born. Two months before his death, John who had seriously considered leaving everything to the children of Charles Quicke at Ashbrittle, who had married an American heiress, bypassed Ernest, and named Edward his heir. The estate was placed in the hands of Sir Redvers Buller, Lord Poltimore and Sir John Shelley as trustees.

Edward and his family had already returned to this country, at the expense of Aunt Fanny, the eldest sister who had married her cousin Nutcombe Quicke and was sufficiently well off to pay for the boy's schooling. By all accounts, Edward was a good-looking dashing young man, a great hunts-man and sportsman, who won the Cresta Run in that last winter before the outbreak of the First World War. He was killed during the first week, at Ypres, acting as messenger because the telephone lines had broken down. His brother Noel narrowly avoided the same fate; as it was he was severely wounded, with the bullet just missing his lungs and was invalided out. He recovered sufficiently to be sent to Egypt where he served until 1920, when he returned home. During his time away he wrote frequently to his mother and his letters describing conditions at the front make interesting, if dis-turbing, reading. What was remarkable was that the postal system remained extremely efficient, and officers could even order food parcels from Harrods to be delivered to them!

On his return, Noel found the estate in a rundown condition. There had been no resident owner since Uncle John's death, and the farms were being inefficiently run by an agent. Noel took a long look at the place, and got rid of the agent. During his brother's tenure, Newton House had been burnt to the ground in 1906. Much of the contents had been saved but it was the trustees who decided upon the architect and the new-style house, and at the same time a major sale of a priceless collection of miniatures to which Christie's devoted a whole day. The new Newton House was equally large and rambling in a kind of Jacobean style.

*Captain Noel Quicke as High Sheriff of Devon 1939–40.*

Courtesy Quicke family

In 1921, Noel married Constance, the daughter of his neighbour Sir John Shelley from Shobrooke. He was fortunately very different from his brother, dull even, and financially prudent, which was fortunate for the estate which he gradually brought back into good order. He always managed to break even and occasionally even have a small surplus. It must have been a considerable struggle for a man never in the best of health with a permanently damaged lung. In 1939 he became High Sheriff; during the Second World War, he was in charge of the Special Constables, and worked tirelessly on various committees. But the extra workload, with his sons both away, told on him and he died in December 1943. It fell to Constance Quicke to keep things going, which she did with only a 'skele-ton staff of ancients' until John the tenth came home.

John had been at New College, Oxford, when war broke out, studying science, and he returned there, but studied agriculture instead, gaining an

MA. As tenancies expired, he took them back 'in hand' and in due course took a long, hard look at the future of dairy farming, deciding to embark on an entirely new venture. He set up a cheese and ice-cream business, using his own milk. This, he thought, would provide a more certain income for the future of the estate, and his family of six children. Quicke's cheeses are now sold all over the country. Mary, the eldest daughter, now runs the business side with her husband. She has taken on her father's mantle, who says that she erupted on the agricultural world in an extraordinary way, and is now an Hon. Fellow the Royal Agricultural Society.

John had married Prudence Berthon in 1953. His mother moved out of Newton to Pulleton, the dower house, where Adelaide had also ended her days, and the Quickes brought up their large family. But in 1967 they decided it was too big, and the increasing volume of traffic using the re-routed road immediately to their rear, was a growing problem. The nearby estate of Sherwood was a much more attractive proposition. This had originally been built for Adrian Cave in 1907 in the Arts & Crafts style, designed by Walter Cave of Sidbury, and occupies a secluded position in a sheltered valley, magnificently planted with trees, rhododendrons and magnolias. John Quicke has always been passionately interested in large-scale gardening and forestry, and for the next few years he and Pru carefully moved their favourite shrubs from Newton to Sherwood. The forestry around Sherwood has been opened up and run in a business-like way providing an income. Old oak coppices have been replaced with Douglas fir, and a policy of small-scale landscaping suited to small-scale farming has been maintained. Sir John considers he manages to employ as many people now as his father did when farming. His eldest son, John, who qualified as a doctor, now runs the forestry side of the estate.

Over the years John Quicke's expertise and deep knowledge has been much in demand. Although he has never been involved in local politics, he has served on the Ministry of Agriculture's Regional Board of which he was Chairman from 1972–75, following this with the Chairmanship of the

*Sir John Quicke.* Express & Echo

Country Landowners Association until 1977, receiving a CBE for his work in this field. He was a natural choice to chair the Countryside Policy Review Panel set up by the Countryside Commission and was knighted in 1988.

The National Trust also has reason to be grateful to Sir John. He served on the Properties & Estates Committee, chairing it in 1984–85 and was awarded an Honorary Doctorate of Science by Exeter University. In 1997, at the age of seventy-five, he retired from everything and now devotes his time to his garden. Sir John never does anything in a haphazard or casual manner. He plants for the future and has acquired a depth of knowledge much sought after by other experts in the world of trees and rhododendrons. There are few more beautiful gardens, especially in the spring and in recent years Sir John and Lady Quicke have opened Sherwood gardens to the public. His younger bother David, who was at one time involved in the family farming and cheese-making business, has an equally fine garden on the edge of Dartmoor and is equally knowledgeable – a remarkable gardening duo. Newton House was split up into flats, and eventually sold.

# ROUS *of Clovelly*

*Clovelly Court before the second fire.*
Courtesy Hon. John Rous

Clovelly is a rare survivor. Feudal villages were once the norm; every great landowner had one; a few even had them removed out of sight! Some were just a huddle of cottages, others purpose-built to house the estate workers. But Clovelly happened over the centuries, beginning at the bottom of that steep and oh so picturesque valley, that is in reality the course of the stream as it tumbles down the cliff to reach the sea. Here grew up a small community of fishermen on land that was part of the manor owned originally by the Giffard family. In the mid-fourteenth century it passed to the Carys from St Giles, near Torrington, and, more famously, from Cockington. It is thought that a manor house existed at this time, also the sturdy quay which survives more or less in its original form and was the basis for the prosperity of the little fishing village which was gradually creeping up the hill.

The manor has been sold only once, but the male line has failed several times, so that the continuity is sometimes difficult to follow. Elizabeth Cary, the last of her line, died in 1730, and in 1738 her husband sold the manor to Zachary Hamlyn from nearby Woolsery.

*Monument to Sir John Hamlyn Williams in Clovelly Church, painted by Lawrence Whistler.*
Courtesy Hon. John Rous

*A sincere Christian, a tender and beneficent Relation, a faithful and kind friend, an inoffensive and cheerful companion… He acquired an handsome fortune not only unenvied, but with esteem and love of all who had the pleasure of knowing him…*

131

…says one hardly impartial account. Zachary was an attorney in Lincoln's Inn. He died unmarried leaving his estates to his five nephews, James, Richard, William, Charles and Zachary Hammett. It was the eldest who changed his name to Hamlyn, a condition of the legacy from his uncle, and is recorded as being 'of Clovelly' and later became the first baronet. Two of his brothers served as Recorders of the Parish. James Hamlyn's wife was Arabella Williams, from Edwinsford, Carmarthen, heiress to her father, and their son added her name becoming Sir James Hamlyn Williams.

It was during the lifetime of the first baronet that the old manor house was burnt down in 1789, together with most of the old deeds and records, so that the early history of the family, and indeed of the village, has many gaps. One wing survived and to this Sir James added a much larger house of the then fashionable Gothic Georgian style. The second Sir James married Diana Whittaker and it was they who were responsible for one of Clovelly's most attractive features, the Hobby Drive. Snaking along the cliff top for three-and-a-half miles, beginning at the lodge gates on the road to Bideford, there are spectacular views out across Bideford Bay, and down to the harbour at Clovelly. Built between 1811–19, Sir James, in common with many landowners of the time, sought to give employment to soldiers and sailors returning from the Napoleonic Wars, impoverished and without any chance of work. Thus, it was called his 'hobby'.

The 1851 census records Clovelly as having a population of 937 – today it is 450. There were around 80 cottages huddled down the main 'street' and the entire village would have been connected with the sea, either as fisher-men or boatbuilders. Many Clovelly men went to sea, deep-water fishing, and some became master mariners, though they never produced a Drake or a Grenville.

Yet again, with the death of the third Sir James, the estate passed via the female line to his daughter Susan, who had married Col Henry Fane, grandson of the ninth earl of Westmorland, and the family adopted the name of Hamlyn Fane. Susan Fane died in 1869, aged forty-five, one year after her husband, leaving their only son, Neville Hamlyn Fane, aged ten to inherit. He was the last direct male heir for over a hundred years, but he died young in 1884 without children, when the estate passed to his remark-able sister, Christine Hamlyn.

Five years after she inherited the Clovelly Estate, Christine Hamlyn married Frederick Gosling, from Hassiobury in Essex. He changed his name to Hamlyn and it was at Clovelly Court that they lived. There were no children. Together they set about restoring and modernising the cot-tages, many of which were in a poor state, and all these bear her initials, CH, and the date of their restoration. She cared deeply and passionately about Clovelly, and was indeed the Lady of the Manor. She is described as having the profile of a Roman emperor, and her diminutive figure was a familiar sight, walking in later life with the aid of a long silver-topped cane. She lived in the grand manner, with Christmas parties for the village chil-dren, and invitations to her house parties were much welcomed, especially

*Christine Hamlyn on her wedding day.*          Courtesy Hon John Rous

in political and artistic circles. Duff Cooper, who married into the Manners family, recalls his first visit in 1907:

> *Mrs Hamlyn came out to greet me and set me completely at ease. She had been left a widow early in middle age and had, I believe, decided to model the rest of her life on that of Queen Victoria. She was dressed entirely in black with a small lace cap on her white hair, so she seemed to me to be a very old lady, although she cannot have been much over fifty. She had an imperious and dominating manner which alarmed nobody. She was a tyrant whom nobody feared and many loved to tease. She had strong political views and was a stern Tory but never allowed her opinions to interfere with her friendships, and Mr Asquith was as welcome at her home as Mr Balfour.*

Raymond Asquith, the eldest son of the Liberal Prime Minister Herbert Asquith, gives an account of one somewhat unusual aspect of a Clovelly house party, recorded on a visit in 1901.

> *It is the custom of the house to plunge en echelon into the Atlantic Ocean as near the centre of it as may be at precisely five minutes before eight every*

*morning. We are rowed out in purple bathing dresses by bronzed descendants of Armada heroes until there is no land in sight but the Island of Lundy and then at a given signal we leap into the blue and bottomless swell and are borne hither and thither like helpless jelly fish in the racing tide.*

*Having sustained ourselves in the waves so long as our strength holds out, we crawl again into the boats and are ferried back to a great lugger anchored off the harbour mouth where we find our clothes elegantly disposed by careful valets; we cover our bodies; light cigarettes and are taken back to land where we find a herd of black thoroughbred Dartmoor ponies; each man and woman selects a mount and we clamber up a sheer precipice where the occasional ash gives a perilous foothold, and so over a rolling park back to the house, where we are welcomed by a smoking mass of lobsters and great dishes of honey and Devonshire cream.*

Raymond Asquith was killed at the Somme. Christine Hamlyn died at the age of eighty in 1936, and with her died the old way of life. This remarkable woman was accorded the village equivalent of a state funeral. Her body lay in state in the parish church for two days, with the tenants mounting a twenty-four hour guard as hundreds of mourners filed past. The funeral service was conducted by the Bishop of Crediton as she was laid to rest in the churchyard with the inscription she had chosen: *I dwell among my own people.*

Constance, her younger sister, married Lord Manners, who is remembered in the family for his success in 1882 when he won a bet to buy, train and ride a Grand National winner, which he did with his horse Seaman. Later that year, for only the second and last time in his life, he raced Lord Chancellor in the Grand Military Gold Cup, which he also won! They lived at Avon Tyrell in Hampshire, which had been Col Fane's home. Mary, their eldest daughter, who would have become lady of the manor succeeding her Aunt Christine, died at Clovelly in 1904 of diphtheria at the age of eighteen. There is a touching memorial to her in the churchyard, beautifully inscribed by Gill: *She sleeps beside the home which has been appointed to her possession, but that God first called her to a greater inheritance.*

A second tragedy occurred when Lord and Lady Manners's son, John, good-looking, a sportsman and everything a son and heir should be, was killed in the first week of the Great War. It is in his memory, as well as other Clovelly servicemen, that the War Memorial was erected at Mount Pleasant, overlooking the village. The younger son, Francis, survived to become Lord Manners.

*Betty Asquith with Mary* (centre) *and her younger sister.*
Courtesy Hon John Rous

It is through the twin daughters of Lady Constance Manners that the history of Clovelly continued. Angela the younger twin, married Col Hore-Ruthven. To Betty Constance, the elder, everything passed on the death of Christine Hamlyn in 1936. She had married the Hon. Arthur Asquith, third son of the Liberal Prime Minister, the First Earl of Oxford. He had a distinguished war record, being awarded the DSO and two Bars, which included service in Greece, where he buried Rupert Brooke, another visitor to Clovelly Court, on the Greek island of Skyros, just before Gallipoli.

Asquith lost a leg in the fighting. He rose to the rank of Brigadier General and collected several other medals for his bravery. After the war he resumed his business career in London and died in 1939.

Clovelly Court had been a Red Cross hospital during the war, and Betty Asquith had just completed a programme of renovation and modernisation when, in 1943, for the second time it was reduced to charred ruins. For nine years Mrs Asquith considered various plans, starting with a new grandiose mansion, but gradually these were whittled down. Her four daughters were all married, and she lived alone, so in the end a small wing was added, and the site of the twice-destroyed house is now a level platform adjoining the oldest portion which, miraculously, survived both fires. John Rous, the current owner, has often considered an extension of his own, for the old house is a warren of small rooms with small windows and he would like a home that takes advantage of its marvellous views.

The Hon. John Rous is the only son of Mary Asquith. The elder daughter of Betty and the Hon. Arthur, she was born in 1919, and married in 1943 as his second wife, the Hon. Keith Rous, second son of the Earl of Stradbroke, a Suffolk family. During the war he had served as a captain in the Royal Navy, and she as a nurse, and in 1946 they moved back down to Penhaven at nearby Parkham. Keith Rous sold his own estate in Norfolk, and with the proceeds bought up farms and land around Parkham and Clovelly. Here the couple brought up John and his three sisters, Caroline, Henrietta and Virginia. But Keith was a restless spirit and eventually he left North Devon to live in Portugal with his common-law wife and third family, leaving Mary to care for her family. The estates were run by trustees up to 1983. Keith Rous returned to this country in the 1970s and in 1983 succeeded his brother as Earl of Stradbroke, a title he held for just four days, before he too died.

Mary Rous is another in a long line of competent and determined women who have cared for the estate and village, ruling with a kindly determination to keep everything together for their heirs. Via Hamlyns, Williams, Fanes and Asquiths, the female line has continued unbroken to John Rous, who in 1984 married Zeenat, an Indian of noble family from Lucknow. They have two daughters, so yet again it will be the female line that will continue to hold this remarkable estate.

Clovelly is now a major tourist attraction with as many as 200,000 visitors each year. The foresighted Christine Hamlyn realised that the number of charabancs bringing visitors to the village were on the increase but few facilities existed. Ironically, the one piece of land she needed for a car park was glebe land, and to purchase it in 1924, she had to sell off other land. John Rous says that without this and her renovations and repairs to the cottages, which made possible the development of tourism, it is doubtful whether Clovelly could have remained in its present state. In the 1970s a major programme of farm amalgamation was embarked upon and some land sales were necessary to finance this. Rents at the time were low and it made sense to consolidate the holdings closer to Clovelly. Today the estate

consists of around 2000 acres including farmland and plenty of 'non-productive woodland' which is outstandingly beautiful, clothing the steep valleys and cliffs. Ancient gnarled oaks have been colonised by rare lichens which thrive in the unpolluted atmosphere. Some return comes in the form of commercial pheasant shoots. Between October and January parties of keen shots fly in from America and the Continent to try their skills in the testing conditions where the birds fly high and fast across the deeply incised valleys. Many of them stay in the two hotels in the village, owned by the estate.

A new visitor centre was built in 1988 to cope with the ever increasing number of visitors, and a major programme of renovation begun. The cottages are old, and maintenance costs are high. It is important to the estate that they are lived in all the year round by local people, many of whom they employ, though in the tourist industry rather than the traditional fishing. A much higher rent could be commanded if they were let to 'incomers' as weekend and holiday cottages, but that would be contrary to everything that Clovelly has ever stood for, and that every successive owner has to striven to maintain.

# SEYMOUR *of Berry Pomeroy*

*Foy pour devoir* – Faith for Duty

*The romantic ruins of Berry Pomeroy Castle.*

The Somerset title is very ancient, granted first to the de Mohun family at the time of the Conqueror, and then to the Beauforts via John of Gaunt and Katherine Swinford, but this line died out in 1471.

The most beautiful and dramatic of Devon's ruins has stood deserted for three-hundred years. Berry Pomeroy was built around the end of the fifteenth century for the ancient Devon family of Pomeroy, or de Pomerais, who had held the manor since at least the twelfth century. Although it occupied a defensive position and was provided with all the usual defence mechanisms such as portcullis, gun loops, steep banks and battlements, there is no evidence that the castle was ever attacked. It stands on a rocky outcrop above the river, overlooking its own deer park, but it is long since that there has been glass in the windows, or deer in the park. The Pomeroys enjoyed its beautiful situation until financial problems forced

*The present, nineteenth, duke, John Michael Edward Seymour.*

them to sell, and in 1547 Berry Pomeroy passed to the Seymour family, who have owned it ever since.

The St Maurs were a Norman family, living in Touraine, and Wido St Maur is generally credited with accompanying Duke William to England. From this beginning, the family is next known in Monmouthshire, where Sir Richard St Mauro built a castle at Penhow. Advantageous marriages followed; his grandson, Sir Roger, married Joan, an heiress of Damerel in Devon around 1335, and in 1358 the sole heiress of John Beauchamp of Hatch Beauchamp, one of the most notable families of the time, married a Seymour. Their son accompanied the Black Prince on his expedition to Gascony, and is the first to be called Seymour.

Sir John Seymour (1474–1536) continued the family's connections with the court. He fought for the king against the Cornish rebels, when he was knighted, and across the Channel in Flanders, and was present at the Field of the Cloth of Gold. He had inherited Wolfhall in Wiltshire from his mother, and served as Sheriff of Dorset, Somerset and Wiltshire. His wife was Marjorie, daughter of Sir Henry Wentworth, who could claim descent from John of Gaunt, so that it is an interesting point that the blood of the original Dukes of Somerset was joined with that of the Seymours. Their three children, Edward, Thomas and Jane, were destined to play prominent roles in the affairs of the times. In 1535, Henry VIII stayed at Wolfhall with the Seymour family, and it was here that he first began to take notice of Jane, who at twenty-six, surprisingly for the times, was unmarried. Edward Seymour, the eldest of the three, was already a respected soldier when his sister married Henry in 1536, and he was immediately created Viscount Beauchamp with lands in Wiltshire at Maiden Bradley, still the family's main home. He became a prominent courtier, and a year later became Earl of Hertford. His sister's death in childbirth did not deter Edward, and he continued to be a trusted general, fighting campaigns against the Scots, including the sack of Edinburgh, and acting as Lieutenant of the Realm in the king's absence abroad. When Henry died in 1547, Edward Seymour manipulated himself into the position of Protector of his young nephew, Edward VI. He was created Duke of Somerset, High Steward of England, Treasurer of the Exchequer and Earl Marshall. However, great positions and wealth bring enemies ever eager to plot, and just two years later Somerset was ousted from power by jealous nobles. During his time in power, Somerset had proved an able administrator, exercising tolerance on religious matters, revaluing the debased coinage, abolishing import duties on corn, and looking to the defence of the realm by repairing the country's fortifications, particularly Calais. He sought to promote peace with Scotland, and hoped to achieve this by marrying the young King Edward to Mary of Scots, which would have been a very shrewd move. However, Mary's French mother would have none of it. Somerset was sent north with an army and heavily defeated the Scots at Musselburgh. In these busy years he found time to build for himself the splendid ducal mansion Somerset House on the banks of the Thames in London, begin a new house at Wolfhall and purchase Berry Pomeroy. But in 1551 it all ended on the scaffold.

Edward Seymour had married Katherine Filliol and their son, also Edward, fought with his father at Musselburgh, and was knighted in 1547. His father's attainder removed all titles and lands, but his son was restored 'in blood' by Act of Parliament in 1553 to inherit manors in Somerset, but not the titles. The dukedom was in abeyance.

But in 1534 his father had divorced Katherine and married Anne Stanhope (who lived to be ninety) and sought to disinherit the children of his first marriage. The dukedom of Somerset was subject to a special remainder to his eldest son by his second marriage, and then to his second son by his first marriage should that line fail, which it did in 1750. From the Protector therefore, two branches of this family existed – the Seymour baronetcy at Berry Pomeroy and Maiden Bradley, and the line of dukes which carried on up to and including the seventh duke. He had no son so on his expiry the dukedom reverted to the Seymours of Berry Pomeroy.

The eldest son of the second marriage, also Edward became dangerously embroiled in the perilous politics of the times with his secret marriage to Lady Catherine Grey, sister of Lady Jane Grey. Though it is Jane who is remembered for losing her head after nine days on the throne, it was Catherine who many thought to be the more rightful claimant all along, a situation not lost on Elizabeth. The couple's marriage, which was deemed to be treason without express permission of the sovereign, came to light when Catherine became pregnant in 1561, and Elizabeth, seeing this as conspiracy against the Crown imprisoned the couple in the Tower, forbidding them to see each other. The birth of their son, Edward, made Elizabeth realise Catherine might seem a more attractive prospect in the eyes of the people, and set out to discredit the marriage. Despite the queen's orders, Catherine became pregnant again while in the Tower and this time, Elizabeth ordered that she and Edward must never meet again, which they never did. Catherine remained in the Tower for much of the next five years, dying of tuberculosis in 1568. Edward was eventually freed, married twice more and lived to be an old man. The couple's first son Edward died before his father, and it was his son, William, who became the second Duke of Somerset when the attainder was reversed in 1660. Supporting the Royalist cause, he fought gallantly for Charles I and was Master of the Household to the Prince of Wales. He secretly married Arabella Stuart, cousin to James I, and was obliged to flee the country, whilst she died insane in the Tower.

The second duke died later in 1660. He was suceeded by his grandson, the third duke, who died unmarried in 1671. The title passed to his uncle, the fourth duke, who died without children in 1675. The fifth duke was shot in Italy by an offended husband in 1678, thus dying umarried at twenty-one. His brother Charles, the sixth duke (and the fifth to hold the title in eighteen years) was known as the Proud Duke and played a major part in the ruthless suppression of Monmouth's uprising in Somerset. He became Speaker of the House of Lords in 1690, and later obtained the post of Master of the King's Horse. The sixth duke was instrumental in securing the Hanoverian succession and married, as her third husband, Lady

Elizabeth Percy, the only child and heir of the Earl of Northumberland, so that their eldest son, Algernon, was not only the seventh Duke of Somerset, but also Lord Percy, Baron Warkworth, Earl of Northumberland, Baron Cockermouth and Earl of Egremont. Algernon was a soldier and took an active part in the Duke of Marlborough's campaigns, whom he served as ADC, seeing action in all the major battles. But he died leaving an only daughter in 1750, when several of his many baronies and earldoms expired. The Northumberland titles passed to his son-in-law, Sir Hugh Smithson; Egremont and Cockermouth to a nephew Charles Wyndham, of Orchard Wyndham in Somerset, and the Somerset title passed back to his distant cousin, Sir Edward Seymour of Berry Pomeroy who became the eighth duke.

When Protector Somerset acquired Berry Pomeroy, he extended the original house, and had he lived, no doubt would have greatly altered the old castle. His son, wisely, made Berry Pomeroy his home and stayed quietly in Devon, out of the limelight. He concentrated on building a grand new house in the Elizabethan style within the original walls. By the time he died in 1593, the Seymour family had achieved a stable position in the county. He had been Sheriff in 1583, had been appointed by Elizabeth I to raise troops to defend the coast against the threat of the Armada, and had quietly consolidated the family's position. His son, another Edward, represented the county in Parliament from 1590–1611, in which year James I created him baronet. With his wife, Elizabeth Champernowne from Dartington, he embarked on ambitious plans for Berry Pomeroy. Were they hoping for a royal visitor to be entertained in the grand suite of rooms built looking out over the deer park? The new wing was far larger and grander than any of the existing buildings, and had as its entrance, a long, classical loggia. The entire third floor was one long gallery, stretching for 207 feet. An estimated £20,000 was spent. It must have been one of the most remarkable, as well as one of the most beautiful houses in Devon of its time, rivalled only by such houses as Longleat, which is considered to have been one source of inspiration to the Seymours.

The third Sir Edward sat through the Long Parliament and fought for his king, being made Governor of Dartmouth in 1644. The town surrendered whilst Seymour was helping defend Exeter, and as part of his fine for supporting the losing side, he forfeited his estates in Wiltshire and Devon. For a time he was kept prisoner in Exeter. He died in 1688 and is buried at Berry Pomeroy.

It was around this time that Berry Pomeroy was abandoned. By 1701 it was already being described as ruinous, and it would seem that the fourth baronet preferred Maiden Bradley because it was closer to London, and that the ancient castle was deliberately demolished, the stonework being sold off to finance a new house at Maiden Bradley, more in keeping with the times.

This Sir Edward made Parliament his career from the age of twenty-seven, continuing until his death. He had a distinguished career, either as Leader of the Opposition or as First Minister, and in 1672 he was unanimously elected as Speaker of the House of Commons, the first time the post had been held by someone not a member of the legal profession.

This influential man, who was head of the Western Alliance of the chief landowners of the West Country, was instrumental in bringing William and Mary over to replace the Catholic James II and was one of those who greeted the Prince of Orange when he landed at Brixham in 1688 Seymour took him to his property near Berry Pomeroy where a form of Parliament was held, before William was conducted to Exeter. Sir Edward lived through four reigns, dying in 1708. His grandson, the sixth baronet of Berry Pomeroy, became eighth Duke of Somerset in 1750. The ninth and tenth dukes were his sons; the latter, inheriting from his brother in 1792, enjoyed the title for only a year before he expired and was suceeded by his eldest son.

The eleventh duke (1775–1855), Edward Adolphus, spent much of his time in Devon. He was an historian, a Fellow of the Royal Society, and of the Royal Literary Fund, and was made a Knight of the Garter by William IV. In 1829 he purchased the Templer's estate of Stover and the Haytor Granite quarries. The family still had interests in Totnes, and the Duke built a stone bridge that opened up a new area of the town where he built over 100 houses for workmen. He also built the Seymour Hotel and the church of St James.

Edward, the twelfth duke, was the second distinguished politician and in 1836 was created the first Earl St Maur of Berry Pomeroy. He sat in Parliament from 1830–55, first as a Conservative for Okehampton in 1830, and then as a Liberal for Totnes from 1834–55, during which time he served as Treasury Lord, Secretary for the East India Board, Under-Secretary at the Home Dept, and Chief Commissioner for Woods and Forests. He was First Lord of the Admiralty from 1856–59, an Elder Brethren of Trinity House, and Lord Lieutenant of the county. He was invested as a Knight of the Garter in 1862. His wife was Jane, the daughter of the playwright, Richard Brinsley Sheridan. Both their sons predeceased the duke, one killed by a bear in India and the other of ill health after fighting for Garibaldi. The twelfth duke died in 1885 when the title passed to two of his brothers in turn, and whose line died out with his nephew the fifteenth duke in 1923.

The title then reverted to the heirs of the eighth duke. His fourth son was the Very Revd Francis, Dean of Wells, whose son had married the widow of a mariner and daughter of a Woolwich publican, and it was his great-grandson, Edward Hamilton (b.1860) who became sixteenth duke. He was educated at Blundell's and Sandhurst, served through various campaigns and the First World War. The seventeenth duke was also a Blundell's and Sandhurst man and a Major with the Wiltshire Rifles, seeing action in the Boer War, and in Aden, before becoming Colonel of the General Staff in the Second World War. His son, the eighteenth duke, was the third to be educated at Blundell's. He married Jane Thomas of Burn Cottage, Bude, and it is their son who inherited as nineteenth duke in 1984.

◇◇◆◇◇

# STUCLEY
## *of Affeton and Hartland Abbey*

### *Bellement et hardiment* – Beautifully and Strong

S ir Hugh Stucley is a very good example of a modest Devon squire, whose ancestry includes several prominent families all of whom have done their duty for the county, all of whom can trace their lineage back at least to the twelfth century.

Centuries of careful and advantageous marriages, a few heiresses and a few descents through the female line, and at the end of it a man combining the blood of the Abbotts, Orchards, Luttrells, Affetons, Bampfyldes, Courtenays, Carews, Chichesters, Monks, Bassets and Stucleys. Sir Hugh is the son of Sir Dennis Stucley, fifth Bt and the Hon. Sheila Bampfylde, daughter of the fourth Lord Poltimore, who inherited the Poltimore estates in North Molton.

The Styeucles originated in Great Stukely in Huntingdonshire, and Richard Styeucle is mentioned as an esquire to Richard II. His wife was the widow of John Bonville (whose son became the first Lord Bonville) and it may

*Affeton Castle.*

have been through her that their son, Hugh, was in possession of lands in Trent in Somerset, and became Sheriff of Devon in 1448, so that he must have had strong connections with the county. His bride was Katherine, daughter and heiress of John Affeton of Affeton Castle near East Worlington, a small village in that part of North Devon south of Exmoor where steeply wooded valleys run down to the rich farmlands of the Exe Valley, and where the landscape and the villages seem to have changed hardly at all over the centuries.

The de Affeton family first emerge in the latter half of the thirteenth century. Affeton itself was a small settlement with a church, mainly consisting of tenant farmers. The de Affetons were perhaps the most prominent. In 1349 plague decimated the population of Devon and it would seem that the village of Affeton virtually disappeared. Nothing remains above ground of the former settlement of Affeton, or of its church, and this very hidden corner of Devon has many secrets to yield up. The de Affetons survived, purchasing their own lands in 1350 and continued to prosper. Over the next fifty years or so they acquired a considerable acreage including the manors of Meshaw, East Worlington and Thelbridge, and by 1370 Thomas de Affeton became High Sheriff, a sure sign of a family's rise up the social ladder. It was his granddaughter, Katherine, who became the eventual heiress of all the Affeton lands, and she married Hugh Stucley.

By this time the Affetons had built for themselves a 'castle' which was more of a fortified manor house rather than a castle in the true sense. This, too, has completely disappeared leaving only the fortified gatehouse constructed by Katherine's son, Nicholas. These were the dark days of the Wars of the Roses, and rival factions could descend at any time without warning on the isolated community so that the gatehouse would have offered some protection. It was described as being over 49ft-high with a spiral staircase and from its top were extensive views, including 13 manors in possession of the Stucley family.

In most old families there is usually one member who is larger than life and the centre of colourful stories, and sometimes something of a 'black sheep'. Sir Hugh, who was High Sheriff in 1544, had two sons. The elder, Lewis, became standard bearer to Queen Elizabeth, but Thomas gained notoriety as an adventurer and a pirate. He must have been possessed of immense charm and a silver tongue for time and time again he wriggled his way out of trouble. It was rumoured that he was one of Henry VIII's offspring, and in 1545 he went with the Duke of Suffolk as standard bearer to the Siege of Boulogne. On his return he became involved in the Duke of Somerset's plot to overthrow the government and, to avoid arrest, Thomas beat a hasty retreat to the court of the French king, Henri II. Foolishly, he returned to England in 1552 when Edward VI had succeeded, with a story that Henri was planning an invasion of Calais. But he was not believed and found himself in the Tower, where he stayed until Edward's death. On his release he was soon in trouble once more, accused of coining false money, and again had to take a hurried departure. This time he went to Savoy and joined the Duke's army. Somehow he wormed his way back into

Elizabeth's favour and persuaded her that he should lead an expedition to colonise Florida. He based himself in Ireland for two years, ostensibly to get together his fleet, but in reality leading a life of piracy of such proportions that it eventually reached his long-suffering monarch's ears and he found himself back in the Tower. Thomas's powers of persuasion somehow managed to obtain his release again and he returned to Ireland where, despite buying himself an estate and being appointed Marshall of Ireland, he returned to his old ways. Summoned to London to answer charges, he again unbelievably managed to clear his name. Home in Ireland he seemed unable to leave his former habits and found himself in Dublin Castle accused of treason and felony. Amazingly, he was let out on the pretext he wanted to clear his name with the queen, but rather than head for London, he fled to Spain, where he adopted the title of Duke of Leinster. Eventually the Spanish court got to hear of Thomas's reputation, and once again Thomas was on the move, this time to Rome and the Pope where he was involved in the victory over the Turks at Lepanto, after which the Pope created Thomas Baron of Ross, Viscount Murrough, Earl of Wrexford and Marquis of Leinster.

Thomas's luck finally ran out in 1578. As a soldier he seems to have been assured of a welcome and he next threw in his lot with the young King Sebastian of Portugal who was mounting an expedition against the Moors of North Africa. Against Thomas's advice, the king insisted on joining battle without allowing his troops time to recover from their sea voyage, and Thomas was killed at the Battle of Alcazar, aged fifty-three.

By the early seventeenth century, the estate had expanded to include most of the neighbouring manors and amounted to 12,000 acres around Affeton alone, but with the succession of Sir Lewis Stucley in 1610, the family fortunes went into decline. Sir Lewis preferred the excitement of life at court and was one of those knighted by James I on his accession to the English throne. In 1618 he was created Vice Admiral for Devon and was given the unwelcome task of arresting Sir Walter Raleigh after his unsuccessful journey to South America to find gold. Despite several attempted escapes, Sir Walter eventually reached the Tower, and his untimely end. So unpopular was Sir Lewis as a result that he was nicknamed Judas Stucley, and he felt compelled to produce a book called *The Vindication of Lewis Stucley* in an attempt to exonerate himself as only doing his duty. In 1621 he also found himself in the Tower for clipping gold coins, a not uncommon practice it would seem, but by then his health was failing and King James let the matter drop. Sir Lewis returned to Devon, to an impoverished estate, shunned by his neighbours, and a year later he died on the island of Lundy, no longer in his right mind. There was very little left for his son, John, who had to mortgage Affeton to the Chichester family for £1000.

The next blow came during the Civil War and it was a body blow from which Affeton was not to recover for a long time. Sir Lewis's son John had managed to hold the estate together despite the problems left by his father, and he had two sons. Thomas the elder married Elizabeth Sydenham, daughter of a prominent Royalist and became involved in the fighting early on, serving as a captain at the Siege of Plymouth. Lewis the younger brother, was an equally active Parliamentarian, becoming chaplain to Cromwell. The unfortunate result of this division of loyalties was that both sides found reason to attack Affeton should they be in the vicinity. The coup de grace was given by Colonel Okey's Parliamentarians, stationed at Great Fulford with orders to mop up and 'reduce' Royalist strongholds; they left Affeton a smoking ruin. Only the shell of the gatehouse remained and the family moved away to Bideford where Lewis married the daughter and co-heir of Robert Dennis, a Bideford merchant. Although they had three sons, it was their daughter, Sarah Stucley whose marriage to George Buck made the next important link in the family chain. The Bucks were a prominent family in Bideford and North Devon, and George as well as being a JP, was elected mayor of Bideford no fewer than seven times. They had a large house known as Daddon and owned a considerable acreage around the town.

Meanwhile, tucked away on the North Devon coast at Hartland, the Abbott family had been quietly prospering. One of the three sons of William Abbott of Luffincott and Hartland, somehow managed to become 'ye Serjeant of ye King's Seller' and he must have done his job exceedingly well for on the Dissolution of Monasteries, Henry VIII granted to William the lands and manor of Hartland Abbey, an ancient foundation set in a sheltered valley remote from almost everywhere. The Abbey is one of those old English properties that have managed to survive for almost ten centuries without ever being sold. It is still lived in by descendants of that same William Abbott, although it has three times passed through the female line.

He was succeeded by his great-nephew, also William, who made few alterations to the old monastic buildings, and who named his three daughters Prudence, Honor and Grace. Prudence, the first heiress, married Andrew Luttrell (d.1625). Even in those days, it seems the Abbey was renowned for its fine gardens, initially inherited from the monks, whose cloisters and monastic walled enclosures survived for several centuries. The Abbey also was very little touched during this period. Despite both Prudence and her

*Hartland Abbey in 1769.*
Courtesy Sir Hugh Stucley Bt

*Paul Orchard the second.*
Courtesy Sir Hugh Stucley Bt

*Anne Orchard, wife of George Buck.*
Courtesy Sir Hugh Stucley Bt

*Sir George Stucley.*

son Nicholas having large families of over ten children, seven of whom died in infancy, three generations later the male line again failed, and Mary Luttrell, the eldest daughter of the last Luttrell, married Paul Orchard from nearby Kilkhampton. She was the second heiress. Little is known of the Orchard family, except that they derived their wealth from their involvement with the Customs and Excise in Exeter, Barnstaple and Bideford. Paul Orchard and Mary set about bringing the Abbey up to date and added a new wing to the south end of the house. Their son, the second Paul Orchard, 1739–1812, made considerable alterations to the Abbey with a grand new suite of rooms, the removal of the great hall and the old cloisters and chapel, and gave the Abbey its distinctive gothic frontage. But he died without children and it was his sister Anne, the third heiress, who by marrying George Buck of Bideford, completed the next important link. (Sarah, the last of the Stucleys of Affeton had married George Buck's grandfather.)

The Buck fortunes were accumulated from trading from the port of Bideford across the Atlantic in cattle, tobacco, timber and salt cod, with around 100 sailings each year, and by the 1750s they had large estates around Bideford and a large house on the outskirts. Bettina, widow of Paul Orchard, lived on at the Abbey until she died at the age of ninety-three in 1833, so Anne and George Buck never moved in, living instead in the Buck mansion of Daddon (later Moreton House), and she died before her sister-in-law in 1820. There has long been a myth in the family that the Abbey was left to Anne Orchard. Sir Hugh recalls his mother looking lovingly at her portrait at the Abbey describing how she had been responsible for planting all the trees in the valley during the long years she lived there. But all the evidence points against this and it was Sir Hugh who, by finding her will kept at the Abbey, exploded the myth. Paul Orchard left Hartland Abbey to his sister Charlotte Hooper Morrison, of Yeo Vale House. She in turn left it to her great-nephew, Lewis William, Anne's grandson.

Anne's only son, also George, who died in 1794 predeceasing his mother, was in possession of the Buck lands, and the Affeton estate which he inherited from his cousin Dennis Stucley, a considerable acreage which ran from Westleigh on the north bank of the Torridge right around Bideford to the coast and included much of this corner of North Devon. It was his son, Lewis William Buck, who eventually succeeded to these two estates and the Hartland Abbey lands on the death of his grandmother. Lewis had a distinguished political career, serving first for Exeter and later for North Devon, spending a total of twenty-eight years at Westminster. There can be little doubt that if he had lived to serve under Disraeli, he would have been made a Minister and ultimately a peer, and this honour was passed instead to his son, George, in 1859 who at that time changed his name to Stucley, becoming Sir George Stucley Stucley Bt. He was fortunate enough to live in that era of settled land and social values when the landed gentry were expected to fulfil various duties and obligations but at the same time had sufficient funds at their disposal to spend lavishly and enjoy a lifestyle enjoyed today only by the seriously wealthy. Sir George fulfilled both roles more than adequately, and it is due to him and his influence that both estates prospered and were dramatically improved.

George had been educated at Eton and Christchurch, Oxford, and was commissioned into the Royal Horse Guards, retiring with the rank of Lieutenant Colonel. He later commanded the Devon Artillery Militia, retiring as Honorary Colonel. He married, in 1835, Lady Elizabeth O'Bryen, daughter of the Marquis of Thomond, a great Irish family who moved in the first circles of society. Sir George and his wife set about bringing Hartland Abbey up to standard with ambitious redecoration schemes which included a set of wall murals painted by Alfred Beer of Exeter, depicting various historic incidents in which the family had been involved. He also imported stone from Malta, which was landed at Hartland Quay, to become the chimneypiece in the billiard room.

In 1855, Sir George, who had been defeated when he stood for Exeter, was returned unopposed for Barnstaple which he served for two terms. He was a controversial MP, changing his allegiance on two occasions, firstly in support of Gladstone's Irish Disestablishment question, and returning over Home Rule. He retired in 1868 and settled into the life of a Devon squire becoming JP, DL and High Sheriff.

Having completed the Abbey to his satisfaction, Sir George turned his attention to Affeton, which had been neglected ever since Cromwell's soldiers devastated it, with just sufficient work carried out to allow it to become a tenanted farm. Sir George repaired the ruined keep and built on a stable wing, so that once again the family could return to this ancient Stucley stronghold.

Sir George had become a keen yachtsman, and in 1870, following the death of his wife Elizabeth, he handed over the Abbey to his son, Lewis. His furniture and possessions were carted down to the little quay at Hartland, loaded onto his yacht and sailed round to the Solent where he rented Exbury House. Probably the most impressive of his many yachts was the RYS *Deerhound* which he purchased in 1868 within four days of first seeing her, and within the next four got together captain, crew, and passengers for an expedition for the opening of the Suez Canal. They arrived in time for the celebrations and were 19th out of a total of 66 vessels to sail through the newly completed canal. The party, which included Sir Stafford Northcote,

*Stucley family group 1859, with* (L to R) *Lewis Stucley, Hugh Stucley, Marion Fane (wife of Lewis, Louisa (wife of Sir George) and Sir George Stucley.*

Courtesy Sir Hugh Stucley Bt

later to become Chancellor of the Exchequer and first Earl of Iddesleigh, were invited to the many celebrations that attended the event.

Later that year Sir George, then aged sixty, married Louisa Granville, twenty-four years his junior. They had two further sons, to add to the three sons and a daughter of his first family, who by then were all grown up. Sir George died in 1900 at Moreton, Bideford. His eldest son, Sir Lewis, succeeded, dying in 1911 when the title passed to his brother, who also died without children. Hugh, Sir George's eldest son, by his second wife, became the fourth baronet, dying in 1956. During much of this time, the Abbey was lived in by Marion Stucley, second wife of Sir Lewis, who only moved out in 1932 when Dennis Stucley, son of the fourth baronet, married the Hon. Sheila Bampfylde, daughter of Lord Poltimore, completing another link in the chain.

Poltimore lies on the outskirts of Exeter, with the decaying manor house clearly visible from the M5 which cuts through its once historic parkland. John Baunfield was styled 'of Poltimore' in King John's time. The family continued to live there and on estates in Somerset. Sir Amias was knighted at Windsor in 1603 by James I and he was buried at North Molton in 1625. His splendid tomb can still be seen in the church. His son married a Drake from Buckland Monachorum and their son, John, MP for Penryn, was created a baronet in 1641. Five years later, Poltimore House was the setting for the surrender of Exeter to the Parliamentarian forces, effectively ending the Royalist cause in the West. He married Gertrude Coplestone, heiress of John Coplestone, another leading Devon family.

*Poltimore House.*

Sir Coplestone Bampfylde, born 1636, was the eldest of 19 children, but fortunately his mother's wealth ensured a reasonable standard of living. Sir Coplestone assisted in the return of King Charles II, presenting a petition to Parliament from the gentlemen of Devon. He must have been a flamboyant character for it was said that 'he fulfilled his duties as High Sheriff with great splendour such as had never been seen before'.

It was Sir George Warwick Bampfylde who was created Baron Poltimore in 1831. He was a courtier and served as Lord in Waiting to Queen Victoria. The family divided their time between Poltimore and the extensive estates on Exmoor where they had a house at North Molton. The second, third and fourth barons followed the family pattern, serving in the Guards regiments and the Yeomanry, riding to hounds and leading a congenial country life. George Wentworth Warwick, the fourth baron had two children by his first wife, his son Coplestone, known as John, and Sheila. John was killed horse racing in 1936, shortly after returning from the Berlin Olympic games where he had been a member of the national fencing team. Lord Poltimore lost heart and for this reason and because of his poor health (arthritis had set in, possibly as a result from a lifetime spent hunting), he made the decision to emigrate to Rhodesia. At the end of the war he sold off all of the Poltimore lands and two-thirds of the Exmoor estate, keeping the North Molton house and lands, which he handed over to his daughter. He never returned to this country and it is said locally that after he left, the rooks of nearby Bampfylde Ring also left for good.

*Lord Poltimore, 2nd Baron.*

Sir Dennis Stucley (d.1983), followed a career in the Guards, was a Major with the Royal Devon Yeomanry Artillery and served as High Sheriff and also played his part in local affairs. He was keenly interested in forestry and was a great sportsman, losing an eye in a shooting accident, which considerably jeopardised his health. He and Lady Stucley divided their time between North Molton, which Sir Dennis preferred because of the sport, and Hartland Abbey, which Lady Stucley preferred because there she created a lovely garden. The couple had four daughters, and one son, Hugh.

Sir Hugh sees Affeton as his family's main seat; they have lived there from at least the fourteenth century and maybe longer, whereas Hartland Abbey is a relative newcomer, only coming into the family in the late 1700s. Moreton House was sold off in 1956 by Sir Dennis; his father had been the last person to make use of it and today it is a boarding school, almost surrounded by the sprawl of Bideford. Sir Hugh followed his father into the Army, serving with the Royal Horse Guards, but now sees himself as basically a farmer. He went to the Agricultural College at Cirencester, and farms the 1000 acres around Affeton 'in hand' which he manages himself 'down to the last nut and bolt'. His eldest son, George, with his brother Peter, run the North Molton estates, including the woodland there, and the shoot. Hartland Abbey and Hartland Quay, which the family have owned since it was built way back by William Abbot between 1586 and 1600, have proved popular with film companies Visitors remember all sorts of strange film sets appearing on the cliffs or around the house.

*Sir Dennis and Lady Stucley with the Emperor of Abysinnia in 1938.*

The Abbey had been let to Highgate School during the war until 1941, and maintaining the house properly had become a constant battle. For a short period through the 1950s, the Stucleys even ran it as a hotel 'which my mother hated' says Sir Hugh. Sir Dennis died in 1983 and it became apparent that some radical rethinking was required. 'The Heritage Trust saved our bacon, without it Hartland Abbey would have had to be sold. Very few people realise what a close run thing it was.'

The house and surrounding land are now within the Heritage scheme and open to the public on a regular basis, and a maintenance fund has been set up to ensure the estate passes seamlessly down to succeeding generations. The Abbey was first opened to the public by Sir Dennis, but the current generation has become much more businesslike about it, opening frequently during the summer season. Sir Hugh's wife, Angela, has a definite penchant for the Abbey, she, too, being a gardener. The house, has been brought up to date and an exciting discovery was the original wall paintings in the dining room, covered over for decades. Part of Sir George Stucley Stucley's grand refurbishment, these depicted the history of the Stucley family and are supposedly inspired by the decorative style employed in the rebuilding of the House of Commons around this time. Yet despite the veneer of so many generations, the old Abbey and its layout can still be traced. The Stucleys still own much of the land around Hartland, farmed by tenants, and there is something of a feudal air here, where change comes very slowly to this remotest part of Devon.

*Sir Hugh and Lady Stucley and their children and daughter-in-law.*
Courtesy Sir Hugh Stucley Bt

◇◇◆◇◇

# WREY *of Tawstock*

## *Le bons temps vindru* – The good times will come

T he earldom of Bath is one of those titles that has been held by several families as fortunes have risen and waned. It has been created, fallen into abeyance, and been recreated and the family to whom it was originally granted in 1536 was older still, for the new earl was John Bourchier, eleventh Baron Fitzwarin. Through his paternal grandmother he was descended from Edward III. That creation became extinct in 1654. The next holders were the Grenvilles, once so prominent in the West Country, who were rewarded for their loyalty to the Royalist cause in 1661. When they died out in 1764 the title devolved through various female heiresses to the Thynne family, created Marquess of Bath in 1789.

*Tawstock Court, Barnstaple, now St Michael's School.*

The Bourchiers claim direct descent from Judhael, son of the Earl of Brittany who was granted the manors of Barum (Barnstaple), Tawstock, Ilfracombe, Totnes, Holne and Dartmouth. Despite the manors being seized by the crown for Judhael's supposed misdemeanours, King Stephen later granted them back again to William de Brewes, great-grandson of Judhael. They were once again seized by King John, and William fled to Ireland where he died in prison of starvation. The lands were granted to Lord de Tracey, husband of William's daughter Matilda. At the end of the thirteenth century, their great-great-grandson married an heiress who brought the manor of Kingsteignton into the family, where it remained until sold in 1744.

A century later, the fifteenth holder of the manor of Tawstock was Margaret, who married Fulke, fourth Lord Fitzwarin. This family could also claim descent from Judhael and had been awarded lands in Shropshire. According to legend, Gwarin, cousin of Judhael and a Welsh Marcher lord, fought a tournament to win the hand of Melette, cousin of William I, defeating the Prince of Wales, the son of the King of Scotland and the Duke of Burgundy, thus winning his bride and Whittington Castle (now part of Ludlow). Their first son was named Fulke and was a close ally of Henry II, their sons being brought up together, and campaigning together. It was Fulke III who figured large in legend as something of a Robin Hood character; having been disinherited by King John, he went into exile and is credited with all kinds of heroic and epic adventures, until his return and restoration under Henry III. The Fitzwarins were created barons in 1292, and it was evidently a title that could pass through the female line, for when Fulke the eleventh (and seventh baron) died childless the title passed to his sister Elizabeth who had married Sir Richard Hankford of Annery, Chief Justice of England. Their daughter, Thomasine, became eighth Baroness Fitzwarin and the ninth holder of the manor of Tawstock. She married Sir William Bourchier, third son of Sir William, who had been created Earl of Eu on his marriage to Lady Anne Plantaganet, daughter of Thomas Duke of Gloucester, son of Edward III and Eleanor Bohun. He was killed at the Battle of Shrewsbury in 1403.

The Bourchiers could also trace their ancestry back to at least the Conquest and were also prominent in affairs of state; Robert Bourchier was appointed Chancellor of England by Edward III, and accompanied him on his campaigns in France. It was his grandson that Thomasine married, and their eldest son was created Earl of Essex. The second son, Thomas, became Archbishop of Canterbury, but the branch died out in the mid-1500s. His daughter married John Mowbray, Duke of Norfolk, so at this time, the Bourchiers were a prominent family, well connected both to royalty and the nobility.

Thomasine and William's son, another Fulke, married a Dynham heiress, and their son married the sister and heiress of the Earl of Bridgwater. It was he who was created the first Earl of Bath, in 1536. He had been a supporter of Henry VIII's desire to divorce Catherine of Aragon, and the king was not unappreciative. Thomasine had manors around Bampton, and Bampton Castle was their main residence, so it was in a chapel attached to Bampton Church that these two generations had their tombs; both castle and chapel have since disappeared.

*Detail from the monument to Sir John Wrey and Blanche Killigrew in Tawstock church.*

The family continued to prosper and to marry well. John, the second earl, married three times, his second wife being Eleanor Manners, daughter of Lord Roos, and a descendant of Edward IV. She was buried at Tawstock, in the aisle built by her husband, but he was buried at the home of his third wife, Lady Margaret Long of Hengrave in Suffolk. This strong-minded lady had been previously married to Sir Thomas Kitson by whom she had a son. Before marrying John Bourchier she drew up careful plans concerning their joint estates, and proposed a double wedding between herself and

John, and her daughter Frances Kitson and his son John Fitzwarin. It was also agreed that the family home was to be Hengrave, not Tawstock. The four of them were married at Hengrave on 11 December 1548. The second earl was frequently away on affairs of state, playing a major role in Mary's accession on the death of her brother, Edward VI in 1553, and accompanying her on her flight to avoid captivity by the Duke of Northumberland, who was attempting to place Lady Jane Grey on the throne. He was rewarded by being made a Privy Councillor and a commissioner at the trial of Lady Jane Grey. Such was his reputation that she entrusted him with keeping the peace as Sheriff in Dorset and Somerset, and made him Lord Lieutenant in both Devon and Cornwall. He cannot have been very much at home at Hengrave, but when he died in 1560 he was buried there in a magnificent marble tomb shared by his wife. His son had died four years previously, prior to the birth of his own son, William, now left in the care of his mother. Although he was brought up at Hengrave, it was during his minority that Tawstock Court was rebuilt if the date of 1574 above the gatehouse is an indication.

Presumably anxious to be free of his grandmother and assert his own will, no sooner had he reached the age of twenty-one than William entered into an improvident marriage with Mary Cornwallis, who was connected to the Kitsons by marriage. The latter were not popular with Lady Fitzwarin, possibly because of their Catholic religion. They were married quietly at Hengrave in December 1577, without her knowledge; two days later William's mother forced a separation, and despite the marriage being found legal by the courts, she was so insistent that eventually it was annulled. Poor Mary was left with her empty title; she was Countess of Bath but nothing else and for the rest of her life was dependant on her family's charity, not dying until 1627.

*The magnificent tomb of the 3rd Earl, William, and his wife Elizabeth.*

William did better with his second choice who was Elizabeth, daughter of the Earl of Bedford, at that time extremely powerful in the county, holding large amounts of land acquired after the Dissolution, and it would appear that his wife was as dominating as both his mother and grandmother had been. Shortly after his marriage, William left for the Netherlands, joining his brother-in-law there in the campaign against the Spanish. Upon his father-in-law's death, William 'inherited' from him at the young age of twenty-nine, the position of Lord Lieutenant of the county. This important post involved the third earl in supervising the defence of the county, especially important in the Armada years of 1587 and '88, when he attended musters of the militia, and supervised press gangs to man the fleet; at this time his deputies were Sir Walter Raleigh, Sir Richard Grenville and Sir John Gilbert, so he was ably supported in his duties. He died in 1623, aged sixty-five; he and his wife Elizabeth share a magnificent marble tomb in Tawstock church.

The fourth earl, Edward, had three daughters by his first wife; his second wife, Ann Lovat, brought the property of Corffe at Tawstock to the family, but no male heir, so that on Edward's death in 1637, the earldom and estates were claimed by Sir Henry Bourchier, who was a grandson of the

*Monument to Rachel, Countess of Bath, in Tavistock Church.*

second earl and Eleanor Manners. His four elder brothers had all pre-deceased him, and he had spent much of his life in Ireland where his father was a soldier. Young Henry attended Dublin University, gaining a BA in 1605 and becoming a Fellow a year later. He was still unmarried at forty-five and there was a suggestion he should marry the dowager countess but instead married Lady Rachel Fane, twenty years his junior.

The fifth earl and his new countess were not left in peace to enjoy their estates for long for Civil War was about to cast its long shadow over the country. Lord Bath did not hesitate but rushed to join his king at York. Control of the militia was vital with both sides haggling over the legality of raising and training bands of men, a duty performed by the Lord Lieutenant, who in Devon was once again the Earl of Bedford, a confirmed Parliamentarian. To counter Parliament's powers, the king issued certain noblemen with 'commissions of array' to oppose such control of the militia, two of whom were Lord Bath and his neighbour Edward Chichester. Lord Bath refused a summons to attend Parliament and was declared a 'delin-quent', to be arrested and his estates sequestered. He spent five months in the Tower, surprisingly was released, whereupon he immediately joined King Charles at Oxford, where he was given the title of Lord Privy Seal. Tawstock Court itself played a pivotal role in the skirmishes and battles surrounding the taking and retaking of Barnstaple, as it held one bank of the River Taw, so Lady Rachel found herself sharing her home with both Royalist and Parliamentarian forces. When it was all over, Lord Bath was fined the comparatively modest sum of £693 for the return of his estates, where he quietly lived out the rest of his life, dying in 1664. Lady Rachel lived on for sixteen years, devoting herself to the relief of the poor, espe-cially the clergy who at this time were thrown out of their livings in large numbers. So effective was she, that on her death the Diocese of Bath and Wells contributed to her marble statue at Tawstock, said by some not to be a likeness of Lady Rachel, but of the Countess of Shrewsbury's effigy in St John's College, Cambridge, which had been made by the same family of sculptors.

As the fifth earl died childless, the earldom fell into abeyance, and the estates passed to the daughters of the fourth earl. The manors of Tawstock and Holne passed to the youngest, Lady Anne, who in 1654 married Sir Chichester Wrey, third baronet of Trebeigh, and they became the 26th owners of the manor of Tawstock.

The Wreys were also of ancient stock, with records going back to 1186 when Robert le Wrey of Wrey married Sybil, daughter of Ralf Abbot. The family remained quiet squires of Devon until in 1596 John Wrey, married Blanche, heiress of Henry Killigrew of Walston, and Trebeigh, which thus came to the family. His son, William, was created the first Baronet of Trebeigh in 1628. He had been High Sheriff of Cornwall in 1612–13 and married a daughter of the third Earl of Devon. Their son married a daughter of the first Viscount Chichester, of Eggesford, later Earls of Donegal, whose son was called Sir Chichester Wrey. He fought on the Royalist side, and after the Restoration became MP for Lostwithiel, and Colonel of the Duke of York's regiment. This is the Chichester Wrey who in 1654 married Anne, daughter and heiress of Edward Bourchier, fourth Earl of Bath. She had been married previously to James, Earl of Middlesex, who is reputed to have disappeared with most of her inheritance. And thus three ancient and important families came together, combining a remarkable lineage.

Anne and Chichester's son was the first to be called Sir Bourchier Wrey, by which title they have been known ever since. He made a significant marriage to a daughter of Sir John Rolle of Stevenstone, another very important Devon family. Like his father he became a Colonel in the Duke of York's regiment, serving in the Netherlands, and was created a Knight of the Bath at Charles II's coronation, and was MP for Liskeard 1688–96. His son also married a Rolle, the daughter of his uncle, John Rolle, and they had nine children. Of his own brothers, one had been killed at Tangiers, aged nineteen, and one killed at Barcelona in 1706.

The eldest son, the sixth baronet, continued the family tradition of military and political service. The seventh baronet married twice; his first wife was a Palk, eldest daughter of Sir Robert Palk of Haldon, who had made a fortune in service with the East India Company. This may have come in useful when Tawstock Court burnt down in 1787 and was rebuilt two years later to fashionable Gothic designs, attributed to Sir Bourchier with help from Sir John Soane.

The eighth baronet, their only son, had an unconventional taste in wives, marrying first in 1818 the nanny to his sister's children, whose husband had disappeared, presumed dead. However, he had the bad taste to turn up again, so Sir Bourchier had to marry his wife all over again in 1832, four years after her first husband had definitely died. His second wife was lady's maid to his first, and daughter of the lodge-keeper on the estate. There are no memorials to these two in Tawstock church. He died in 1826 to be succeeded by his half-brother, the Revd Sir Henry Bourchier Wrey, rector of Tawstock, who died 1882.

*Sir Robert Bourchier Wrey, 11th Bt.*

The eleventh baronet, Sir Robert, was the last to live at Tawstock Court and to keep house in the old manner. He was a JP and Deputy Lieutenant, and had a varied career, serving first as a captain in the Royal Navy and Royal Defence Force; he was made a Major and Hon. Col in the Royal North Devon Hussars, and was decorated for his part in the Zulu, Egyptian, Burmese and Chinese campaigns. He did not marry until he was fifty, and died in 1917 aged sixty-two, leaving an only daughter, Rachel. Sir Robert was one of a large family of eight sons and six daughters; four of his brothers inherited in turn, the second, Sir Philip, having two daughters; the third, the Revd Sir Albany, rector of Tawstock, had no children; the fourth had a distinguished military career in Egypt and China but neither he nor his two younger brothers had children, so it was the son of the seventh brother, Edward Castell who eventually became the fourteenth baronet and thirty-seventh holder of the manor of Tawstock. Richard Bourchier Wrey, born 1903 was initially a naval man, invalided out in 1940 but continuing to serve in the RNVR. In 1973, Sir Bourchier and his wife moved to South Africa, her former home.

The North Devon estate, up until the early twentieth century, had remained almost intact. It stretched from Ilfracombe down to Umberleigh and was around 13,000 acres. The Wreys had large holdings in Ilfracombe and built the first pier, which they partially rebuilt and enlarged in 1760. Here they had a manor house overlooking the harbour, so they must have had considerable shipping interests at that time. Their principal home was always at Tawstock Court, a large Elizabethan mansion overlooking the River Taw, which burnt down in 1787, when many of the family records and possessions were also destroyed. Only the medieval gatehouse remains of this earlier house. Sir Robert (eleventh baronet) by all accounts overspent his income, having no son to inherit he was not interested in preserving the estates. Even in his lifetime he found the expense of Tawstock Court too much, and moved out to Corffe, letting the house, which later became a boys' preparatory school. October 1919 saw the break up of the estates; some 2500 acres went under the auctioneer's hammer, many farms being sold to the tenants, realising the sum of £67,000.

What was left when the fourteenth Sir Bourchier inherited was the nucleus of the estate surrounding Tawstock on the outskirts of Barnstaple, around 7000 acres. By the 1970s, this, too, had gone and Tawstock Court itself had been sold to the school which remains in occupation. Sir George Bourchier Wrey, the fifteenth baronet found himself with a few-hundred acres and one farmhouse, in which he and his family live and run a property business entirely unconnected with the estate they once owned. He believes firmly that you must look forward, not back, and it is no good regretting the loss of the family estate, but still says it could have been a valuable entity to have retained the 7000 acres, and a worthwhile thing to have run economically. There is very little left of the family possessions, so much having been sold off first by Sir Robert and then by his own father, but some of the ancestors still remain in the parish of Tawstock on the walls of the farmhouse, and in the church where some of the most interesting memorials in the county, to the ancestors of the Fitzwarins, the Bourchier Earls of Bath, and the Wrey families are to be seen.

# YARDE-BULLER *of Churston*

## *Aquila non capit musca* – The eagle does not catch flies

The Yarde-Buller family, in common with the Downes of Crediton, descend from James Buller of Morval, in Cornwall, and therefore from Bishop Trelawny whose daughter he had married. Three generations later, Francis Buller laid the foundations of the Yarde-Bullers by marrying an heiress, Susannah Yarde. Francis was an eminent lawyer and in 1778 was appointed to the King's Bench, and to the Court of Common Pleas in 1794, by which time he had been created a baronet. Susannah inherited the estates of her father at Ottery St Mary and at Churston Ferrers, near Brixham, where the Yarde family had lived for several generations at Churston Court, close by the church. Their only son, Francis, became the second baronet, dying in 1833. Of his two sons, the younger, Edward, founded the Manningham-Buller family, later Viscounts Dilhorne, and John, the elder became Baron Churston, at the end of a parliamentary career which had spanned more than a quarter of a century. He had represented South Devon from 1835 until 1858.

The old house of the Yardes was considered old-fashioned and not grand enough, so when the opportunity came to purchase nearby Lupton House in 1840, formerly home of the Hayne family, Sir John took it, and called upon George Wightwick to remodel the Palladian mansion. Lupton was

*Lupton House.*

*Lord Churston, 2nd Baron.*

*The beautiful Yarde-Buller sisters who took Society by storm.*

again remodelled following a major fire in 1926, without its top storey, and without the Salvin additions of 1862. Neither house is still in the ownership of the family.

The first baron's son died before his father, (both married daughters of Edward Sacheverell Chandos Pole), but not before he produced a large and interesting family. John (the third) inherited as the second Baron Churston and served with the Scottish Fusiliers. Geoffrey, the third son, was sent to South America to 'better himself', which he did by marrying in 1919 Hortensia, the daughter of an Argentinian nobleman. Their eldest son was known as Senor Norberto Yarde-Buller of Buenos Aires, where his descendants still live. Geoffrey had 14 children by two wives, and an enormous number of grandchildren, so that there are probably more Yarde-Bullers in South America than in England.

The fourth son, Henry, was a distinguished soldier and diplomat, and was much decorated for his part in many campaigns which included the Nile Expedition, Crete, the South African war and the First World War. He served as Military Attaché in most of the capitals of Europe, headed various missions on the Continent, and was knighted in 1917. The fifth son became a canon of Truro Cathedral. Bertha, the only daughter, married Sir Lopes Massey Lopes.

The third baron, John, MVO and OBE, was a soldier like his father and grandfather, serving with the Scots Guards. He was ADC to the Viceroy of India in 1902–03, and to HRH Duke of Connaught 1904–06, and was decorated for his part in the South African War. However, when he fell in love with, and ultimately in 1907 married, Denise Orme, an actress and singer, his military career was over for he was obliged to resign his commission. He was recalled at the outbreak of the First World War when his soldiering capabilities were considered more important than his mesalliance.

Denise Orme may not have been good enough for the Scots Guards, but she produced a remarkable family. She had two sons and four daughters, born between 1908 and 1918. Such was their beauty that her daughters took Society by storm when they were 'presented' between the Wars. The youngest, Primrose, married the seventh Earl of Cadogan; Denise became Lady Ebury; Lydia married the Duke of Bedford; and Joan, the eldest, married Loel Guinness. The latter's daughter Victoria married Stavros Niarchos, and Joan's second husband, whom she married in 1936, divorcing in 1949, was Prince Aly Khan. It is her son, Karim, who is the present Aga Khan, and who also chose an English bride, Sally Crocker-Pole. This is a remarkable tally, and their remarkable mother, who divorced Lord Churston in 1928, went on to marry as her third husband, the Duke of Leinster as his third wife in 1946. She died in 1960.

Described by her son-in-law, the Duke of Bedford, as 'one of the most fabulous and enchanting characters I have ever met', she was born Jessie Smithers, daughter of a judge's clerk. As Denise Orme, she was one of the principal attractions at the Alhambra, Leicester Square, where she used to sing 'No one ever wants to marry me'! Her second husband was a Dane, Tito Wessel and, after they divorced, Denise ran a private hotel in her house, Beech Hill, in Sussex. It was here that Lydia, recovering after her first husband was killed in action, met the Duke of Bedford, also recovering from the death of his first wife. Denise, he recalls, was wonderfully hospitable, but forgetful; she would invite people to lunch, or dinner, and then forget all about it, so that when they duly turned up, nothing was prepared for them. When she thought it time for her guests to leave, she would approach them, pull them to their feet, shake them by the hand and say what a shame it was you had to go, but do please come again! Such was her charm, that they always did. The engagement between Lydia and John Russell, then the Marquess of Tavistock, was announced the same day as the marriage took place, to keep the ceremony as quiet as possible. To escape the daunting family relationships that bedevilled so many generations of the Russells, the Tavistocks decamped to South Africa, where their son, Lord Francis, was born in 1948, only returning 'with deep foreboding' to Woburn on the death of the twelfth duke in 1953 as a result of a shooting accident whilst staying at Endsleigh, the Russell house near Tavistock.

*Denise Orme, wife of the 3rd Lord Churston.*

The couple moved to the gloomy, antiquated mansion and it was the Duke's idea to open Woburn as a serious money-making proposition. Lydia was faced with the Herculean task of refurbishing Woburn after two generations of neglect. Everything was filthy and shambolic; the Sèvres dinner service given by Louis XV to the fourth duke, found boxed up in one of the stables, was washed by Lydia herself, and it seemed the whole house was one large antique treasure chest. Woburn first opened to the public in 1955, after two years of unrelenting hard work. It was Lydia who arranged the main rooms and the result was 'as if someone had waved a magic wand and Woburn had suddenly become a happy home'. The Duke gives Lydia much of the credit for the Woburn success story. It was on that first open day that one of the visitors pressed a sixpenny piece into Lydia's hand, saying, 'And that's for you ducks'. The Bedfords bought a house in Jersey where they escaped with their extended family, both having two children from their previous marriages, and Lydia brought them all up as one happy family. Eventually, however, the couple divorced.

The eldest brother of all those lovely sisters was Richard, who inherited as fourth Lord Churston in 1930. A Lloyd's underwriter before the war, he served in the Navy and after the war decided to sell much of the property in South Devon, including Lupton Court, and moved to Guernsey.

For John Francis, his eldest son, and the fifth baron, Churston Court was never more than a holiday home, the family's main bases being Guernsey, or London. He decided to sell off Churston and look for a more modest estate in a quieter part of Devon, and settled on a house near Tiverton. Lord Churston, a former stockbroker, and his Spanish wife, Alexandra Joanna, spend some of their time here, but the family has a cosmopolitan lifestyle with relations all over the world, and he maintains his links with both the family of the Aga Khan, his cousin, and his Greek relatives.

# Bibliography

The standard works without which no history of Devon families could be completed include:

Burke's *Landed Gentry*. (various editions).
Burke's *Peerage, Baronetage, and Knightage* (various editions).
*Country Life* (which has included numerous articles on Devon country houses during the twentieth century).
Hoskins, W.G.  *Devon* (1954).
Lyons, S. & D.  *Devonshire* (1822).
Polwhele, R.  *The History of Devonshire* (1793–1806)
Prince, J.  *The Worthies of Devon*  (1801 edn).
Snell, F.J.  *Devonshire*  (Mate's County Series, 1907).
*Transactions of the Devonhire Association.*

In addition there a number of specialist monographs, the more important or entertaining of which include:

Acland, Ann.  *A Devon Family: the story of the Aclands* (1981).
Austin, Dr A.  *Clinton Family – A History of the Clinton Barony.*
Chichester, Alex P.B.  *History of the Family of Chichester* (1871).
Chape, R.P.  *The Book of Hartland* (1940).
Clifford, Hugh.  *The House of Clifford* (1987).
                *Compton Castle, Devon* (National Trust, 1979).
Cruwys, M.C.S.  *A Cruwys Morchard Notebook, 1066–1874* (1939).
                *The Devon Carys* (1920)
Fletcher, Ronald.  *The Parkers of Saltram* (1970).
Fortescue, Hugh.  *A Chronicle of Castle Hill, 1454–1918* (1929).
Fulford, Francis.  *Bearing Up.*
Gore Allen, W.  *John Heathcoat and his Heritage* (1958).
Locke, A. Audrey.  *The Seymour Family* (1911).
Parkinson, C. Northcote.  *Edward Pellew, Viscount Exmouth.*
Pepys, Paulina.  *Powderham Castle: the historic home of the Courtenay family (1980 edn).*